How to be Smart, Shrewd & Cunning --Legally!

How to be Smart, Shrewd & Cunning --Legally!

Courthouse Secrets of judges and top trial lawyers revealed to show you how to avoid misfortune, win disputes, boost self-confidence and laugh all the way to the bank

Richard Lee Orey

To order additional copies of this book, contact:
Xlibris
1-888-795-4274
www.Xlibris.com
Orders@Xlibris.com
591083

CONTENTS

Acknowledgement and Dedication

For the foundation that permitted me to create this book, I was gifted with in-depth personal and professional associations with courtroom giants—

> Honorable Charles Briggle,
> Judge, United States District Court
> Springfield, Illinois

> and

> Honorable George Lazar,
> Honorable Clarence Harden,
> Honorable Donald Meloche,
> Judges, California Superior Court,
> San Diego, California
> and

> Melvin Belli, Esquire,
> Trial Lawyer and Legal Scholar Extraordinaire.
> San Francisco, California

I recognize with admiration their comprehensive legal knowledge, wisdom, and long-standing encouragement and support that enabled me to bring this work to you.

Dr. Eric Berne's revealing book *Games People Play* describes a game we all need to prepare for . . .

"Now I've Got You, You Son of a Bitch!"

How to be Smart, Shrewd & Cunning—Legally! is your survival guide for our shark-infested world.

—Richard Lee Orey

Introduction

We all want to be honest, responsible citizens. We all want to preserve and build our assets. And we all want to avoid personal and professional misfortunes.

When we have a sore throat, we know what to do. We gargle with aspirin for relief. When we have chest pain and difficulty breathing, we know we have a problem but we don't know what to do, so we waste no time in seeing our medical advisor.

But oftentimes in this shark-infested world, we don't recognize we have a legal problem in our personal or professional lives until we're in over our heads. While hiring a lawyer may be the smart thing to do to help you make the right decision on everyday personal activities and business relations if you've got lots of cash, most of us don't have the resources to maintain a lawyer on a monthly retainer. *How to be Smart, Shrewd and Cunning—Legally!* explains fundamental legal principles and offers simple examples so you can recognize risk exposures and potential legal pitfalls in your everyday affairs—oftentimes even before they arise—so you'll know when to seek professional legal advice and how to cooperate most effectively with your legal practitioner.

By devoting focused attention to the text, hypothetical situations and pivotal secret keys I've lifted from my legal education, thirty-eight years of courtroom trial experience and close association with top legal professionals and shared in this book, you will acquire personal knowledge that will enable you to avoid legal misfortunes, win legal disputes, take charge of your life and oftentimes laugh all the way to the bank in many everyday situations that otherwise might prove for you to be financially devastating with possible criminal liability.

The presentations in the named chapters and the other prominent sections in this book are offered for the purpose of providing you with upgraded personal information on broad concepts of generally accepted legal theories and principles, on structure and basic procedural functions in the American judicial system and for the purpose of outlining and providing general study guides of legal information helpful in your everyday affairs. The information provided in this self-help manual has not been presented and should not be taken in any way as advice and counsel on any specific legal problem or issue. You should consult an appropriate legal professional such as a State-licensed attorney-at-law in good standing in local and state Bar associations on any significant matter relating to your personal or business legal affairs.

Mastering the legal know-how in *How to be Smart, Shrewd & Cunning—Legally!* will not make you a lawyer, but it will provide you with specific "insider" legal knowledge well beyond the level of the typical citizen and will give you the advantage of recognizing and structuring in advance a multitude of transactional issues in our society, as well as providing you a sound platform in selecting and communicating with your legal professional. Bear in mind the adage *A little knowledge is a dangerous thing* and an admonition bandied about among lawyers, themselves: *A lawyer who represents himself has a fool for a client.* If you have a legal problem, consult with your lawyer!

How to be Smart, Shrewd & Cunning—Legally! allows you the freedom to study at your own pace, keeping in mind that there are four main learning chapters and that devoting one week to each learning chapter and its Review and Workshop sections will allow you to cover, review and quiz yourself on all the material within thirty days. In your first thirty days of study, you will acquire a great familiarity with the material presented. But it would be unreasonable to expect that within thirty days you will have mastered the material. Be patient with yourself. Persistent study, quizzing and review will bring you great rewards!

I would bring to your attention that there is a commonality of material in the chapter devoted to Tort Law (Injuries to Person and Property) and the chapter devoted to Criminal Law (Punishable Conduct) in that many acts described in a chapter may be the subject of both a possible criminal prosecution by law enforcement officers and the subject of a civil lawsuit for damages by the victim of any particular act. One example is that a woman who has been sexually assaulted and raped may learn that the rapist has been charged and is being prosecuted for the criminal act of rape even as the rape victim, herself, sues the rapist in a civil lawsuit for money damages for her personal injury and emotional distress.

Let me point out that how you use the courthouse secrets revealed in *How to be Smart, Shrewd & Cunning—Legally!* in your everyday personal and professional life is entirely up to you, including that once you "own" the legal savvy presented, you'll have the option of acting Smart, Shrewd and Cunning—Legally!

Be Prudent. Take Care.

CHAPTER ONE

Justice

I want to tell you a story that can change your life. One hot summer's morning as young Eve Adams walked along a downtown sidewalk, she noticed a book propped up against the pole of a street light. Picking up the book, she read its title: *How to be Smart, Shrewd & Cunning—Legally! Courthouse Secrets to avoid misfortune, win disputes, boost self-confidence and laugh all the way to the bank.*

The fortunes of life had left Eve divorced with two young children, homeless, jobless and broke. When she got divorced, she knew nothing about her community property or child support rights. When she got evicted from her apartment, she didn't know about her eviction notice rights or how to get the return of her security deposit. When she got pressured out of her job by a bullying supervisor, no one mentioned wrongful termination or unemployment rights. The weight of all her life struggles and the fact that she didn't know where to turn or how to make things better had left Eve Adams seriously depressed.

Eve read the book title, again. *Avoid misfortunes? Win disputes?* Sounds too good to be true. *Laugh all the way to the bank?* I don't even have a checking account anymore!"

Eve wasn't sure what the words meant. But as her eyes confronted the printing on the following paragraphs and pages, she knew the words were meant specifically for her. These are the words I wrote to her and that I'm sharing now with you:

My name is Richard Lee Orey. As an official court officer, I sat daily in federal, state and municipal courtrooms for thirty-eight years listening to every word of testimony and legal arguments as I participated in more than six hundred jury trials and tens of thousands of criminal, civil and domestic abuse cases and secret grand jury investigations on subjects ranging from first degree murder to contract disputes to child abuse.

Because of my unique professional background, I've appeared as a paid keynote speaker in over two hundred law-related educational seminars and as guest lecturer in trial and discovery procedures for numerous professional and educational institutions, including the University of San Diego School of Law and the California Western University School of Law.

From my legal education, courtroom experience and close associations with judges and top trial lawyers, I've stockpiled a virtual warehouse of practical legal know-how and courthouse secrets. In this book, I'm going to share valuable parts of that legal savvy with you.

You're single and on your own, now, Eve. As you journey through life alone, you're going to face many personal challenges affecting your legal rights having to do with child support, labor disputes at your employment, contract disputes with your local department store and automobile accidents and other negligence issues and even criminal charges that might be filed against you over bounced checks or driving with alcohol on your breath.

Eve, the practical legal knowledge in this book is the first step of getting you back on your feet. To live a secure and comfortable life, it's essential for you to know how to protect yourself and how to safeguard your personal and property interests. If you want equality in treatment and justice in your life, it's important that you know how to recognize challenges to your personal and property interests and how to deal with them in an effective and legal manner.

The first thing I want to share with you is to tell you that in our country, personal justice is guaranteed by the proper administration of law, especially by the determination of rights according to duly enacted rules of law and rules of equity.

So, Eve Adams, do you want to get back on your feet? Do you want to take control of your life? Do you want to master your fate?

Yeah, Richard. Tell me what I need to know.

This is going to take more than a few minutes, Eve. So, I suggest you and all you others reading these words walk over to that park down the block and pick out a nice spot where you can sit on the lawn and rest your back against a shade tree.

Okay, Richard. I'm on my way. Just keep talking.

I will. And let me say, also, that at the end of this first chapter of my sharing of legal savvy here with you, you'll find a few pages titled Justice Review. Putting in a little time studying those pages and the following Justice Workshop will be very helpful. But pay attention because getting back on your feet starts right now. This is Day One!

Eve, the first thing I want to share with you and everyone else is that our country is blessed with a supreme rulebook called the Constitution of the United States and its Bill of Rights. Any disputes and challenges between citizens of this country seeking justice are decided by reference to legally enforceable rights under the rules outlined in our Constitution.

The responsibility for administering those rules of justice in our United States Government is divided into the three governmental branches: The Legislative branch, the Executive branch and the Judicial branch.

Today, I'm going to talk with you about the administration of justice from a practical and personal standpoint, Eve. Listen closely because you're going to learn about the grass roots administration of justice provided by the Judicial branch.

Before I talk with you about specific laws that affect you with regard to contracts and agreements and disputes and accidents and intentional injuries and criminal acts and various legal responsibilities of you and others you come in contact with, let me talk with you about our system of courts so that you'll have a background and overall understanding of our American judicial system.

In basketball or in baseball, when you play in your own gymnasium or ball park, that's termed your home field advantage. That's your home base. In Law, *Jurisdiction* is the term which denotes your home base, that is, which court is involved with the responsibility of deciding which cases. On the question of jurisdiction of the courts, let's talk first about state courts or the court system within an individual state.

Courts function with two categories: One is an *Appellate* structure and the other is a *Trial* structure. Taking it from the top down, there will be a highest court in the state, usually known as a Supreme Court, although the names will vary in the various states. This is the highest Appellate Court within the state. Because of the sheer volume of appeals filed, that Appellate Court cannot rule on appeals in all cases, so it has an assisting or helper court. This is the lower level of the appellate system and that is usually known as a Court of Appeal.

If you have to go to court and you lose your case and want to appeal from a trial court decision, your case will go directly to a Court of Appeal, from which you may even later appeal to the Supreme Court.

But let's not get the cart before the horse, Eve. Let's talk, first, about our local trial courts. There is usually one trial court within a state with a helper court. The trial court is commonly known as a Superior Court (including Family Court and Juvenile Court) but sometimes is known by other names, such as a District or Circuit Court. This is the trial court for all matters involving large amounts of money or involving felonies or serious criminal charges. A Superior, District or Circuit Court has a helper court usually known as Municipal Court.

A Municipal Court tries civil matters with a limited jurisdiction, such as $15,000 on civil trials or issues of tenancy and eviction. It will also try misdemeanor criminal cases such as petty theft and shoplifting, and the judge therein will act from time to time as a magistrate or a preliminary hearing judge on felonies to decide whether or not there has been a crime committed that is a felony and that the defendant is likely to be guilty. If so, then that defendant would be held over for trial in the Superior Court.

The Municipal Court quite often is known as a court of the people because it is often on a grass roots level. It is close to your community but, by virtue of this, has an enormous volume of business. And so it has a branch within it usually designated as a Small Claims Court. In some jurisdictions, Municipal Courts are being phased out in favor of one Superior Court with internal divisions such as Traffic Court and Juvenile Court. Small Claims Court usually has the same judges who hear cases involving less than $25,000.

So, Richard, if I loaned someone, say, $200 and they didn't pay me back, is that where I would go for help?

Yes. That's exactly what the Small Claims Court is for. Later on, we'll talk in detail about that. I'm sure you've also heard the expression, *Don't make a federal case about it.* By that, the person is referring to what is termed a federal issue or a matter that is not proper for a local Municipal or State Court but comes within the jurisdiction of a Federal Court.

So, let's talk about the federal court system. The federal court system is a system of limited jurisdiction. It will not hear a case at all unless there are certain very strict guidelines which have been complied with.

At the top of the list of the federal courts we have, as we all know, the United States Supreme Court which, again, because of volume of business cannot hear appeals in all cases. It has helper courts: United States Courts of Appeal. These Courts of Appeal are located in districts through the United States. The federal court system, also, has a trial court: the United States District Court."

You may ask, *How will I know when to go to federal court?* The answer is that when the matters at issue involve a federal law or a federal officer or residents of different states, the matter will be heard in the federal court system and tried in the United States District Court.

Now, there are some special exceptions to this because of volume of business. As an example, there has been created a specialized court called the United States Bankruptcy Court which deals just with matters involving bankruptcies. And then the United States Tax Court, which involves itself with matters purely on tax appeals.

In the state courts insofar as jurisdiction, one can say that the state court has jurisdiction over any subject matter not exclusively reserved to a federal court, so long as either a party or the subject property is resident within the state.

The federal court, on the other hand, takes jurisdiction only when the issue presented to the court involves a federal law or federal officer or federal property or is a conflict between states or citizens of various states (known as diversity).

You mean like if I get in a car accident with someone in another state?

Exactly, Eve. But sometimes it's not always clear. You remember that I mentioned the word *jurisdiction?* Well, when a matter is brought before a court, the first issue that the court must decide is whether or not it has authority or power to hear the case. The first issue before any court, therefore, is *jurisdiction.* A court always has jurisdiction to hear and determine its own jurisdiction.

Put another way, when you file a lawsuit in a court, a judge of that court does have authority to hear the theory of the case, the basic facts of the case, in order to decide whether or not it has the authority to try the case on its merits.

Let's talk a little bit about how lawsuits get started. A case comes before a court by reason of an initiating legal paper being filed. We'll talk about, first, a civil action. The paper being filed which starts or initiates a lawsuit is called in most courts a Complaint. A Complaint is a written statement of that which you complain, naming the person that you have a dispute with or that you believe caused you an injury.

That person then is summoned into court. A Summons is issued to that person which tells them, "You have to respond to this written Complaint or the person that is complaining—usually called the Plaintiff—may take a Judgment against you and execute or collect on that Judgment."

So, if you're summoned into court, Eve, you must file an Answer, a written denial or an admission. As a practical matter, if you are sued, if you receive a Summons through the mail or in person that tells you that you have been sued, you must respond. You should contact a lawyer immediately. Do not delay. Every day is important. Take all the court papers with you when you go.

Now, if you're arrested by a police officer, give your name and give your address but nothing else. Do not discuss the facts with the police officer or anybody else. Ask for a lawyer immediately.

In criminal cases, my experience of almost forty years in the court systems reveals that in at least three-fourths of the cases where a conviction thereafter results, the persons arrested have either convicted themselves or substantially assisted the prosecuting authorities by one thing: Talking to the authorities and discussing the facts of case. Even though the persons arrested have been admonished of their right to remain silent and not to say one thing, the persons invariably talk, anyway. **Give your name and where you live.** But other than that, **Don't talk.**

Ask for a lawyer or your own lawyer.

Now, when I talk about getting a lawyer or calling a lawyer, I should first mention that you should have a lawyer already. Don't wait until a problem arises, especially if you own and operate a business.

If you don't have a lawyer at this time, I suggest that this is part of the program of getting back on your feet. Make contact with a lawyer.

How do I get a lawyer, Richard?

If you don't already know a lawyer, a business associate that you have reasonable confidence in most likely does know a lawyer. Ask for their recommendation.

If you don't want to do this or you are not satisfied with their recommendation, go to your local Bar association. Take out your telephone book and look under the name of your county such as Los Angeles County Bar Association. Most Bar associations have a lawyer referral service. Call the Bar association and tell them, "I want a lawyer on a business problem I have" or "I was arrested on a criminal charge and need a lawyer."

The Bar association representative will give you a name or names and contact information of a lawyer in your local area that specializes in your type problem or a lawyer who has experience in your legal problem.

Right now when you have no legal problem is the best time to search out a lawyer experienced in family law or business affairs. Contact that lawyer. Arrange for a preliminary visit in his/her office just to get acquainted so the lawyer will know the nature of your personal and business affairs. Then when a problem does arise, you can save time by contacting your own lawyer.

And if your problem is of a particular nature—say, you've been arrested for driving under the influence of alcohol or a drug—your lawyer is prepared to represent you without delay or can refer you promptly to a lawyer that is experienced in your particular problem.

One fact of life: If you want to get fast action from a lawyer, be prepared to put money on deposit for the lawyer's services, often called a retainer: "Here's $500 as a retainer. I need representation right now."

When you pay up front, you will get prompt action. But always ask for an itemized billing for all services rendered.

Now that we've talked about getting a lawyer, let's talk about what a lawyer will do for you as far as the court system is concerned.

First, know that lawyers deal with initiating or defending legal actions, civil or criminal. Lawyers deal with the presentation of evidence, matters that can win your case.

Evidence is divided into four general categories:

Oral evidence, that is, the sworn testimony of witnesses.

Physical evidence, that is, exhibits, documents, contracts, photographs, rifles, products, anything that is physical.

Another category that is treated as evidence is a stipulation. This is an agreement between the lawyers. This eliminates the necessity of bringing in certain evidence if they can both agree on a certain fact. In a courtroom this agreement must be approved by the judge.

A fourth category of evidence is Judicial Notice. Some things are so universally accepted that you don't have to present evidence to prove it exists: The world is round. California is a state within the United States.

Evidence is that which your attorney has the responsibility to introduce in a court to support your legal position. The opposing lawyer will be presenting evidence that will be contra or opposite to your position. Your lawyer will try to stop or block the introduction of that evidence.

The main thing that you will be involved with is oral evidence, that is, testifying.

Now, if you are involved in litigation, that is, civil litigation such as a business lawsuit, you will be involved in two areas of giving testimony: Deposition and Trial.

A deposition is a statement that you will give under oath before trial, most likely in a lawyer's office. You will be placed under oath by a notary public, and the lawyers—usually the opposing lawyer—will ask you questions.

After you have answered all the questions of the other lawyer, your attorney may, also, ask you questions, almost always simply to clarify any answer you've given.

Your testimony at this time will be reported word-for-word by a certified court reporter and later reduced to a typewritten transcript.

The other time that you will be testifying is at the trial in the courtroom. It is important for you to know at the time of your deposition that you may later be testifying on the same subject matters in a courtroom and before a judge and jury. Know this: Your deposition testimony has the same force and effect as if it were given in a courtroom. And if you change your testimony at trial from that given in a deposition, the opposing lawyer can point this out to the judge and jury and perhaps discredit you and your case.

Now, I want to give you Ten Commandments for testifying. It doesn't matter whether you're testifying in a lawsuit that you brought or a lawsuit that someone brought against you or even as a defendant in a criminal charge filed against you.

These are ten important rules you should always follow when testifying.

1. *Tell the truth.*
    If you tell the truth and tell it accurately, nobody can cross you up.

2. *Don't guess.*
    If you don't know, say you don't know.

3. *Understand the question.*
    You can't give a truthful and accurate answer unless you understand the question. If you don't understand the question, ask to have the question repeated or rephrased.

4. *Take your time in answering.*
    Listen to each question individually, formulate your answer, then state your answer.

5. *Give a clear, audible answer.*
    Talk loudly and clearly so everyone can hear and understand you. Don't nod or shake your head.

6. *Don't look around for help.*
    Look at the person asking you the questions. Don't look to your lawyer or the judge for assistance.

7. *Beware of time and distance.*
    If you make an estimate, make sure everyone understands you are estimating. Don't guess.

8. *Be polite.*
    Answer questions with *Yes, sir* or *No, sir.* Address the judge as *Your Honor.*
    Don't argue or fence with the lawyer on the other side.

9. *Admit preparatory conversations.*
    If asked whether you have discussed the case with anyone before testifying (such as with your lawyer or an investigator), admit it freely, if you have done so.

10. *Avoid jokes and wisecracks.*
    A lawsuit is a serious matter. Smart answers or remarks may well jeopardize your case.

Now, let me tell you how to answer questions:

1. Listen to the question.
2. Answer the question asked:
    a. From your attorney: Freely and openly.
    b. From the other attorney: Directly. Make your answer as short as possible. Don't volunteer.

Limit your answers:

Unless you are asked and permitted to explain something, there are only six possible answers that you should give:

1. Yes, sir.
2. No, sir.
3. I don't know.
4. I don't remember.
5. I don't understand.
6. The relation of a fact:
   About ten feet.
   In June, 1995.
   It was a 4-door Chevrolet.

Don't volunteer.

You can help your lawyer help you by doing certain things.

Number One, tell your lawyer when you first visit him all the facts about your case. Don't withhold anything. Don't put your lawyer in the position of being surprised in court.

Your lawyer functions under professional ethics and a professional law. He cannot reveal what you stated to him as your lawyer in confidence to anyone else without your permission. It's like going to a priest in confession. He cannot reveal it. If he does, then you can sue him for damages. And he's aware of this. Not only that, he's ethically bound. He wants to represent you.

How can you help your lawyer? Tell him everything. Preserve all evidence. Don't throw anything away. Secondly, when you first see your lawyer or as soon as you can, try to organize all the evidence.

Now I have provided for you in the Workshop section of this chapter a suggested style of evidence summary to prepare and to give to your lawyer. This summary provides, for example, the dates that certain things happened and any document or any notation or anything that will subthstantiate that.

For example, "On August 10, I went down to a restaurant in Mexico City." And if you happen to have a book of matches from that restaurant, preserve it and refer to that item in your evidence summary. It may not be helpful or it may. That's not for you to judge. Just preserve it and organize it if you can along the lines of the suggested Evidence Summary I have provided.

Now, the purpose in bringing a lawsuit is to obtain a judgment; and in defending a lawsuit, you also want to obtain a judgment. Let's talk about the two kinds of judgments that apply.

In a criminal case, you can obtain a judgment of acquittal. This means that the trier of fact—be it a jury or a judge—finds you not guilty, and that ends the case.

Another kind of trial result could be a "hung jury." The jury is just unable to decide. As an example, in a criminal case, it takes a vote of all the jurors finding you guilty beyond a reasonable doubt. If you have a jury of twelve people, and eight of them think you are guilty and four think you are not guilty and they are unable to resolve it any further, then you have a "hung jury," and the matter undoubtedly will be tried again.

Then you can have a judgment of conviction. The jury finds you guilty, and the court accepts that, having reviewed the verdict and seen that it is proper in form. That then is a judgment of conviction.

Three things can happen after that. Upon conviction, you can receive probation in a criminal matter. That means that you will be reporting to a supervising probation officer for a given period of time, say, six months or thirty-six months, or you can be sentenced to serve a period of time in custody in a state prison or in a county jail.

Now, sometimes on your sentencing you will be given probation but will have to serve a specified period of time in custody as a condition of probation. As an example, you're sentenced to three years in state prison with the execution of the sentence being suspended for a period of three years while you are placed on probation for that time on condition that you serve the first six months in the custody of the sheriff in the local jail.

No matter what kind of conviction is returned against you, you have the right to appeal. You can take your matter to a higher court. When your matter reaches a higher court, the judges or justices there are not going to review your matter to see whether or not ab initio or from the beginning you are guilty or not guilty. They'll just look to see whether or not there was sufficient evidence to support the jury's finding, that is, was it reasonable that the jury found so and so.

Secondly, the judges or justices are going to review the matter to see if any errors of law were committed that would materially affect your defense or your prosecution. Were there errors of law that would affect the outcome of the case? If there were, the matter will be remanded back to the trial court for a new trial.

Now, let's talk about what happens in a civil matter.

In a civil lawsuit, the loser is going to have to pay. Either he is going to have to pay by doing what the plaintiff wanted him to do or, more likely, he's going to have to pay money. He's going to have to pay for damages and attorney's fees, et cetera, or at least the plaintiff's costs in bringing the suit.

Now, he can do two things at that time: Number One, he can appeal his matter to a higher court and/or he can negotiate a settlement after the judgment is entered. In other words, you can have a judgment entered against you of $200,000, and you can appeal that judgment to a higher court and—while the appeal is pending—you can negotiate with the attorneys on the other side to settle the matter at a lesser amount than the judgment.

The other side to your lawsuit doesn't know when you appeal to a higher court that they are going to be successful. They're hoping that the judgment they have against you will be affirmed, but they don't know. So, if you pursue the matter, you may be able to effect a compromise settlement of the judgment against you.

If you are the winner of a judgment in a civil lawsuit, you can collect your money judgment by way of a Writ of Execution whereby a local law enforcement officer—likely the marshal of the court—will go out and "tap the till" of the defendant. Also, you can negotiate a settlement.

You have a judgment of $100,000 and, rather than have the defendant appeal the matter and try to evade your execution, perhaps he will agree to pay you upfront right now, especially if it's in a reduced amount.

Now, in a civil case, if you are a winner and the defendant has appealed the case and you do not want to negotiate a settlement, you are going to have to respond to the appeal.

If on appeal the Appellate Court affirms or approves your judgment from the trial court, then you can execute the judgment. You can go out and collect it. And you are going to receive not only your money judgment but are entitled to accrued interest on your judgment from the time the judgment was entered initially by the trial court.

If on appeal, however, your judgment against the defendant is reversed, you lose. Either you have lost everything or your matter may be remanded for a new trial, in which case you have to go through the function of another trial or, perhaps, you can negotiate a settlement.

Now, one can say that lawsuits are won in the courtroom, but that's not the whole truth. The key to winning lawsuits is as simple as A-B-C:

Preserve the evidence.
Initially, when things are going on and everything is fresh, preserve the evidence.

Organize the evidence.
Have every document, every item, every date completely itemized and cross-referenced with all the other items of evidence.

Present the evidence.
Presenting the evidence will be a simplified matter if you have preserved everything and you have organized everything. In that event, you are either going to win your lawsuit or, even if you are in the wrong, you are either going to win or defeat the main thrust of your opposition's case.

In many respects, a lawsuit is similar to parliamentary procedure. If you've done your homework, really have prepared and you know what you're doing, you can tie up anybody or get accomplished almost anything you want—if you have out-prepared, out-organized and equally present the evidence as the other side.

In summary, with one exception, when it comes to the administration of justice, let your lawyer do the talking. When you utilize the services of a lawyer, it's the same as using the services of your accountant or your medical doctor. The same principle applies: They will analyze the situation for you and make professional recommendations. But you are going to be the one that decides what to do.

I suggest that you should follow the recommendations of the professional that you have chosen and let your professional do the acting out.

To that, there is one exception: When you have a matter pending before a Small Claims Court—such as when you sue to recover rent or a security deposit or some damage to an item of your property in the amount of, for instance, $300 or $400, which comes within the jurisdiction of the Small Claims Court—you may not have a lawyer present and representing you in that courtroom. You must present all matters yourself.

Now, while your lawyer cannot represent you in the Small Claims courtroom, you may consult with your lawyer all you want before entering the courtroom. So, you may get his advice on how to proceed before you try your Small Claims lawsuit.

So, Number One, there are no lawyers involved in a Small Claims lawsuit, but it's okay to consult a lawyer beforehand.

Also, there are certain limits in Small Claims lawsuits. In many states there is a maximum financial limit of, for example, $7,500. Now, if you have a claim above that level—say, $10,000—you can sue in that court but you have to limit your claim to $7,500, and you'll have to waive the excess of your claim above the $7,500 limit, which may be worth it to you rather than to file your claim in the Municipal Court and endure many delays.

Additionally, the defendant must be served a notice. That's a procedural matter that you must follow in filing the Small Claims Court lawsuit. You must serve the defendant a formal notice that he is being sued.

In most jurisdictions, notice by certified mail is proper so long as you ask for and receive a receipt. You will need to present that receipt in court before you can proceed with presenting your case to prove to the judge in the courtroom that the defendant was, in fact, served with a Summons to appear.

You can also have the defendant served with notice, personally. Personal service by any individual is proper so long as the person serving the summons is not a party to your lawsuit. The server can be your brother, or your good friend can serve the notice on the defendant.

Now, if you really want to get the attention of the defendant, have your local law enforcement official serve your Summons to Appear on the Defendant. In California, that official would be the Marshal, the law enforcement officer of the Municipal Court.

There's something quite intimidating and highly suggestive of getting prompt action when a person in uniform wearing a law enforcement badge knocks on the defendant's door and says, "You have been served. Here is a Summons to Appear in Small Claims Court.

When you get your money judgment in the Small Claims Court, the judgment just sits there for awhile. You cannot force the defendant to make payment. There is a waiting period. In California, as an example, that waiting period is twenty days, during which the defendant can pay you or he can file an appeal.

Now that twenty days doesn't have to be lost time. If you won a judgment, you can spend that time locating the defendant's assets on which you might later execute, such as his car or his bank account.

If you're the losing defendant, you can use that twenty days' time to somewhat restructure your assets in order to maintain a low profile. This is not to suggest that you hide your assets in order to avoid execution of judgment by the plaintiff, but it may be convenient from a business standpoint in order to conduct your business that you transfer certain assets from one name to another name or transfer your operating cash from one bank where you usually maintain it to an account in another bank.

Now, when it comes time to execute on your Small Claims money judgment, that is, to go out and collect it, once an appeal is filed, there can be no execution at that time. You have to wait the time for the defendant to appeal.

If the judgment is not appealed, the Clerk of the Court will issue a Writ, a formal legal paper, which you may hand to a Marshal of the Court to go out and collect the money for you. But you have to tell the Marshal where to go. He will not go out and search. You have to tell him where the plaintiff's car is and a detailed description of it or where the defendant's bank account is: what bank and under what name. Then the marshal will go out and collect your money.

In conclusion, whether you are handling the matter or your lawyer, remember this: The key to winning lawsuits is to preserve all the evidence, to organize all the evidence, and then—either you or your lawyer—present the evidence in a simple, logical manner.

In the administration of justice, the best thing you can learn is to conduct your business with intelligence and with the knowledge you have learned in this self-help training manual and with your lawyer.

But remember this: Your lawyer is your agent, your assistant. You are in charge.

This sharing of legal knowledge in the administration of justice has been for the purpose of acquainting you with broad concepts of generally accepted legal theories and principles and of the structure and basic procedural functions in the American judicial system. The information provided in this self-help manual has not been presented and should not be taken in any way as advice and counsel on any specific legal problem or issue.

You acquired this book so that you could become become smart, shrewd and cunning—legally! Well, you're on your way. To continue moving down that pathway, I want you to spend some time reviewing the Justice Review section on the following pages, which will tie together and add to much of the general overview information I've been talking about in this first section. To quiz yourself after your Review, next go to the Justice Workshop section.

Justice Review

RESPONSIBILITY OF GOVERNMENT BRANCHES

Legislative   Executive   Judicial

JUDICIAL BRANCH

State Courts
Supreme Court (Top appeal)

Federal Courts
U.S. Supreme Court

Court of Appeal (Lower appeal)

U.S. Court of Appeal
(Numbered circuits plus
District of Columbia)

Superior/District/Circuit
(Trial Court)

U.S. District Court
(Trial Court)

Municipal Court (Lower trial)
Small Claims Court

Bankruptcy Court
U.S. Tax Court

HOW JUDGES ARE SELECTED

Elected
(Between elections, vacancies
are filled by appointment of
State Governor)

Appointed by U.S. President
(Nominated AND
Confirmed by
U.S. Senate)

HOW PROSECUTORS ARE SELECTED

Attorney General (State)
(Elected)

U.S. Attorney General
(Appointed by President)

District Attorney (County)   U.S. District Attorney
(Elected)   (Appointed by President)

City Attorney
(Elected)

JURISDICTION OF COURTS

State Courts
Subject Matter:
Any issue not exclusively
federal

Federal Courts
Subject Matter:
Federal Statute or Code
Federal Question—
Interpretation of U.S.
Constitution or regulations:
Bankruptcy, Admiralty

Parties:
At least one party a state
resident

Parties:
Federal officer or issue between
states or Diverse Citizens:
(Example: Arizona resident sues
Florida resident)

Property:
Located within state:
(Real estate, car, bank
account)

Property:
Federal property: (truck, money,
real estate, etc.)

FIRST ISSUE BEFORE ANY COURT:

Jurisdiction

A court always has jurisdiction to hear and determine its own jurisdiction.

Removal:
A case is taken out of State Court and into Federal Court

Remanded:
A case is sent back to the State Court for lack of Federal jurisdiction.

Dismissed:
A case filed improperly in Federal Court

(Example: Case between citizens of same state with no issue of Federal law or property.)

PLEADINGS AND PRETRIAL PROCEEDINGS

CIVIL

COMPLAINT:
Initiating document filed by Plaintiff

SUMMONS
Notifies Defendant he/she is being sued

Demurrer:
"So what" statement by Defendant to Complaint
(Even if you believe everything in the Complaint, it doesn't state a triable cause of action against Defendant.)

Motion to strike:
Filed by Defendant alleging Plaintiff's Complaint is a sham or names improper parties or says there is a surplus of pleadings.

ANSWER
The Defendant denies or admits the allegations of the Plaintiff's Complaint

CROSS-COMPLAINT
A cross-suit filed by the Defendant

ANSWER TO CROSS-COMPLAINT
Plaintiff's "Answer" to Defendant's cross-suit

AT ISSUE MEMORANDUM
States the issues between the parties are joined.
The matter is ready for trial.

DISCOVERY

PHYSICAL
Property and person

ORAL
Parties and Witnesses appear at a "Deposition"

Notice:
A party must appear. Witnesses are subpoenaed.

Signature:
A person who testifies at a deposition later signs the typewritten transcript of his oral testimony given at the deposition.

MOTIONS

Summary Judgment
A motion filed by the Defendant to dismiss the case.
The Court determines: "Is there a triable issue?"
Yes—Denies the motion. No—Grants the motion

READINESS-SETTLEMENT CONFERENCE
Can the parties settle the case?
Is the case ready for trial?

CRIMINAL

Felony:
The *possible* punishment is Death or State Prison

Misdemeanor:
The *possible* punishment is only local custody up to one year.

PRELIMINARY HEARING RE FELONY:

    Municipal (City) Court: GRAND JURY
                                      (Federal or County)

Complaint	Presentation of evidence by
Arraignment	Prosecutor
Entry of plea: Guilty/Not Guilty	

Preliminary Examination:	Grand Jury action:
Discharge of Defendant	No Bill
Defendant Held to Answer	True Bill (Indictment)

A transcript of all oral testimony in a Preliminary Hearing/ Grand Jury proceeding will be provided to the Defendant and the matter proceeds to appropriate trial court.

TRIAL COURT

Charging "Information" is filed by the prosecutor	Indictment is presented to court by the Grand Jury

Defendant is arraigned (told of the charge)
and enters a plea of Not Guilty/Guilty

MOTIONS

To **Suppress Evidence** (Example: for illegal search)

To **Quash Indictment** (Example: insufficient evidence)

Demurrer
Legally disqualifies charge (Example: Grand Jury exceeded its authority or facts alleged, if true, constitute legal excuse or justification)

READINESS-SETTLEMENT CONFERENCE
Plea bargain to settle case (Example: Prosecutor will reduce charge in exchange for Defendant's guilty plea)

Ready for trial?

THE TRIAL

Challenges and Motions
Challenge Judge as biased. Defendant asks for different judge.

Motion in Limine: (Before trial begins)
To suppress evidence

Challenge to array:
Defendant alleges entire jury panel was not called or selected properly.

VOIR DIRE
Questioning of jurors: "Can you be a fair and impartial juror in this case?"

Peremptory Challenge: No reason given. Juror dismissed.

For cause Challenge: Juror found to be biased. Dismissed.

OPENING STATEMENTS to trier of fact: Judge or Jury
By the Plaintiff: "The evidence will show..."
By the Defendant: "The evidence will show..."

The Plaintiff gives his opening statement first.
The Defendant may give his opening statement next or
Reserve and give his opening statement at the beginning of the Defendant's evidence.

EVIDENCE
Legally admissible proof on a disputed issue. To be admissible, all proof must be *relevant,* that is, it must tend to prove or disprove a matter in issue.

Kinds of Evidence:
1. Oral statements of witnesses
2. Judicial Notice by the Court (accepts commonly known fact).
3. Exhibits: Documents, objects
4. Stipulations/statements of agreement by parties

BURDENS OF PROOF:
Civil:
Preponderance of evidence
Clear and Convincing (fraud issues)

Criminal:
Beyond a reasonable doubt

RULES OF ORDER OF EVIDENCE

Plaintiff:	**Defendant**
Presents oral evidence and introduces exhibits	Cross-examines witnesses and objects to testimony/exhibits

Special:
In a Civil trial, the defendant may be called as a witness by the Plaintiff.

In a Criminal trial, the defendant may testify in his own case, but he may not be called by the prosecutor to testify.

Motions:
At the end of the Plaintiff's case, the defendant may move for a "non-suit" on the ground of insufficient evidence by the Plaintiff, that is, that the Plaintiff has not made out a prima facie or basic case, and asks the Judge to take the matter away from the jury and dismiss the case.

Judgment: In a non-jury case, the Defendant may ask the judge to weigh the evidence even before the Defendant puts on his evidence and decide the case now.

The Defendant asks the judge to advise the jury what verdict should be returned. In a Criminal case, the defendant wants the judge to discharge and release the Defendant.

TRIAL
In a Criminal case, the trial proceeds in the same manner as in a Civil case (above).

When both parties have "rested" their presentation of evidence, the parties will confer with the judge as to the Instructions the Judge will give to the jury regarding how the jury will proceed to deliberate and arrive at a verdict.

At the conclusion of the presentation of the evidence:
The Plaintiff/Prosecutor will give his Closing Argument:
"This is what the evidence means…"

The Defendant will give his Closing Argument:
"This is what the evidence means…"

The Plaintiff/Prosecutor may then give a Rebuttal argument to refute any new matters raised in argument by the Defendant.

The Judge instructs the jury on the law of the case.

JURY VERDICTS

Civil:
A specific number of jurors must agree on the verdict: Usually 9 of 12.

Criminal:
All jurors must agree unanimously to the same verdict: Guilty or Not Guilty.

(There can never be an *undecided* vote by a juror. The vote is always in favor of the defendant in a civil case until a juror is satisfied by a preponderance of the evidence that the Plaintiff has proved its case and a vote for Not Guilty in a criminal case until a juror is satisfied *beyond a reasonable doubt* of the guilt of the Defendant.)

POST TRIAL

MOTIONS:
Civil:
By the Plaintiff to tax or to be reimbursed its costs of suit.
By the Defendant for new trial.

Criminal:
Pronouncement of judgment:
Sentencing or Probation

Appeal:
The Losing party may appeal the verdict to a higher court which will review the legal issues involved at the trial.

Notices of Appeal:
Civil: Deposits money with the Clerk for the cost of the court reporter's preparation of a verbatim transcript of the oral proceedings at trial.

Criminal: Files notice of appeal. Transcript will be provided at government expense.

SUGGESTED STYLE OF EVIDENCE SUMMARY TO PREPARE AND GIVE TO YOUR LAWYER

DATE	EVENT
2010, Jan 10	Bought 2009 Ford from Browne Motors
Feb. 10	Left fender fell off of Ford while parking.
Feb. 12	Mr. Jones at Browne Motors refused to repair the fender.
Mar 15	Engine blew up on Ford while drive down city street
Mar. 20	Asked Mr. Jones at Browne Motors to repair the engine. Mr. Jones told me, "Sorry. Engine repair is not covered by your warranty."

Documents:

1. Sales agreement and warranty when buying the 2009 Ford from Browne Motors
2. Photo of Ford on January 10 right after purchase
3. Photo of Ford on February 11, one day after fender fell off.
4. Photo of engine compartment of Ford on March 15 after engine blew apart.

Justice Workshop

QUESTION 1
What is the first issue before any court?
Answer: _____

QUESTION 2
An indictment (or presentment) is issued by what body?
Answer: _____

QUESTION 3
You are parked near an intersection, and a post office truck crashes into the side of your car and damages your car and severely injures you. If you sue for money damages, in what court should you file your lawsuit?
Answer: _____

QUESTION 4
What is the name of the initiating paper or pleading that you file with the clerk of a court to begin a lawsuit?
Answer: _____

QUESTION 5:
What is the name of the procedure during which a judge and the attorneys ask questions of jurors?
Answer: _____

QUESTION 6
In the courtroom in front of a judge, the two attorneys announce they agree to a certain fact. What is the name of that agreement?
Answer: _____

QUESTION 7
In a trial, what is the name of the party that ordinarily calls the first witness to testify?

Answer: _____

QUESTION 8

In a civil trial based on the claim of negligence, the Plaintiff must prove its case by a preponderance of the evidence.
What is that standard called?
Answer: _____

QUESTION 9

You have been served with a document titled "The Superior Court. Complaint" which announces that you have been sued. In order to defend yourself in the lawsuit, you must file a document that denies the claims made.
What is the name of that document?
Answer: _____

QUESTION 10

You have been called to testify in a lawsuit between a company and a former employee where the issue is a non-competition clause. If you testify first in a lawyer's office before trial, that is called a what?
Answer: _____

QUESTION 11

I loaned my neighbor $350 six months ago, and now he refuses to pay. If I want to sue him to collect my money, what court may I file my claim in?
Answer: _____

QUESTION 12

What is the name of the court where you may not be represented by a lawyer?
Answer: _____

QUESTION 13

After winning a judgment against a defendant, you may have a law enforcement officer go to his place of business and take money out of his cash register. All you have to do is ask for a Writ of _____.

CHAPTER TWO

Contract Law
Promises and Agreements

I'm going to share with you now what you need to know about promises and agreements and contractual obligations, what is commonly known as Contract Law.

WHAT IS A CONTRACT?

A contract is a promise by one person to another, for sufficient consideration, which creates an obligation to do or not to do a particular thing.

A contract is a legally enforceable promise or agreement.

I say, *Jim, I've admired your manufacturing plant for many years. I would like to buy it. I'll give you one million dollars in cash for it on the first of next month.*

Two weeks later, I say, *Jim, I know we wrote our agreement down on this piece of paper, but this is what I'm going to do with that.*

And I tear up the paper and say, *Jim, we don't have an agreement anymore. The deal is off. We don't have a contract anymore.*

Jim tells me, *Oh, yes, we do.*
And why? Because Jim knows a **contract is not a piece of paper.**

You see, writing down our agreement helps us not to forget what the terms are of our agreement. It is the written memorial of our agreement or promises. The piece of paper is evidence of our agreement. Tearing up the piece of paper does not end the agreement. It only affects the written evidence of our agreement.

Save the pieces of paper for your lawyer.

Here's something to remember: Just because a paper document says *Contract* doesn't mean it is a contract.

Example:
Billy Smith loves to kick a football.
His friend Lucy says, *I'll hold the football for you, Billy.*
Billy says, *Do you promise you won't drop the football on me like you always do?*
And Lucy says, *Yes, I promise, Billy.*
Well, Billy comes up to kick the football, swings his leg and just at that moment Lucy drops the football. Billy swings his leg free, misses the football and drops on his rear, embarrassed.
Lucy is laughing hysterically at Billy's foolishness.
Billy feels humiliated. He's going to see his lawyer and sue Lucy for breaking her promise.
Billy's lawyer says, *Let me look at this situation from the standpoint of my legal training, Billy.*
And Billy's lawyer does, applying his legal training like this:

Every enforceable agreement or contract is formed or based on Elements

Element Number One, you have to have **competent parties**; that is, are the parties sane? Are they of the age of majority so they are held responsible under the law?

Element Number Two, is there a **lawful object**; that is, is the subject of the agreement not a criminal act or not an act contrary to public policy but something that is acceptable in the eyes of the law?

Element Number Three, is there an **offer**, that is, a conditional promise? Did you offer Lucy something in exchange for her promise?

Element Number Four, did Lucy accept the offer, an unequivocal **acceptance**: Yes.

Element Number Five, was there **consideration;** that is, was there an incentive for Lucy? Was there an inducement, a quid pro quo, a something-for-something that makes this an enforceable contract?

Example:

Billy, the lawyer says, *in looking at this last element of consideration, what we have in this situation is not a contract because there is no consideration for Lucy's promise. So, you have no basis on which to sue Lucy for her breach of contract.*

If you had promised to give Lucy your chocolate pudding if she would hold the football for you and she agreed and she failed to hold the football, then you would have fulfilled the necessary element of consideration to support an enforceable contractual agreement.

To understand **consideration,** let's discuss kinds of contracts and talk about them as three groups.

First, let's talk about **unilateral** and **bilateral** agreements. These two kinds of contracts refer to promises.

UNILATERAL CONTRACT (One party has yet to perform)
Example:
I go to a Jeep dealer, and I say, *Here's my check for $18,000. I want to buy a Jeep.*

The dealer says, *I have no Jeep in stock right now, but I promise to deliver one to you on the fifth of next month.*

You say, *Okay.*

This is a **unilateral** agreement. Only one party has yet to perform.

BILATERAL CONTRACT (Both parties have yet to perform)
Example:
I go to a Jeep dealer and say, *I want to buy a Jeep. On the fifth of next month I will pay you $18,000 for a Jeep.*

The Jeep dealer says, *Okay. Unfortunately, I have no Jeep in stock right now, but I promise to deliver one to you on the fifth of next month And you say, Okay. That works for me.*

This is a **bilateral** agreement. Both parties have yet to perform.

NOW, let's talk about express and implied agreements.

EXPRESS AGREEMENT:
In this kind of agreement, the terms are specific and stated:

Examples:
Jim, the charge is $5 a gallon OR On June the tenth OR $2.95 a pound.

IMPLIED AGREEMENT:
In this kind of agreement, the terms are *not* specifically stated but are implied.

Example:
You visit your medical doctor, and you do not ask him in advance, *What is your fee for an office call?* It is implied that he will charge you a fee and that the fee will be a reasonable fee.

NOW, let's talk about a third classification of contracts or agreements, a classification that refers to performance.

Remember this: A contract is either *executory* or *executed.*

EXECUTORY or EXECUTED CONTRACT:
When we're talking about an *Executory* contract, we're talking about incomplete performance.

Example:
I have already given the Jeep dealer my $18,000 payment for the Jeep, but he has not yet performed his promise by delivering to me a Jeep.

On my part of the agreement, I have completed or executed my performance, so as to me, the agreement is *executed.*

On the dealer's part of the agreement, he has yet to complete or execute his performance, namely, delivering to me a Jeep. As to the dealer, this contract is *executory.*

Here's a special notation: From time to time you may hear someone talk about the fact that he *executed* the contract when in fact he's talking about putting his signature on a document setting forth your agreement. His statement is not accurate. You sign a contract or sign an agreement. *Executed* refers to performance of the terms of the agreement.

Now, let's talk about:

FORMATION OF A CONTRACT. A major issue in litigating a business lawsuit in the courtroom has to do with contract formation.

To better understand your rights, let's talk about enforcing an agreement or contract AND let's talk about breaking an agreement or contract.

OFFER:

The Number One thing in the formation of a contract is that you must have an *offer*. The person who makes the offer is the *Offeror*.

There are 3 things to remember here:

1. The *Offeror* has to intend to be bound.
   I'll give you one million dollars for your second-hand bicycle.
   That's obviously a joke. The **Offeror** did not intend to be bound.

2. The terms must be definite and certain.
   If there is a dispute and you go into the courtroom, the judge has to be to able to calculate or fix the obligation. He has to be able to know what it is that you agreed upon, such as, *I'll pay you $220 on March 1st for your Sony voice recorder, Serial No. 22855.*

3. The offer by the **Offeror** has to be *communicated* to the **Offeree,** the person that he wants to accept the offer, not to a stranger.

Example:

It doesn't do any good for me to tell Bill that I will give Jim one Million dollars for his manufacturing plant if Bill is a stranger and doesn't even know Jim. I must give the offer directly to Jim, the person I want to accept it (or to his authorized agent).

ACCEPTANCE:

We have made an offer. Now, what about the acceptance? Let's talk in two areas, first.

1. *Assent to terms.* You accept a contract by saying *Yes* either in words or by deed, such as doing something like signing your name.

A *grumbling acceptance* is a major issue in court. A grumbling acceptance says this, in effect: *Yes, but...*

Yes, I accept your deal, but I think it's highway robbery, and I'm going to report you to the Better Business Bureau. Everything after the word *Yes* is immaterial.

2. **Communicated** to the Offeror.

If I want to accept a contract, I have to do it in a timely fashion.

If I receive an offer in First Class mail, then I must respond in First Class mail or in some way as fast or faster.

Common Business Practice: I have to respond as fast or faster than the person did who offered me the job, who offered me the agreement, who offered me the contract.

The Mail Box Rule: When someone makes you an offer through the mail, you may respond by placing a written response into the United States mail, properly addressed and with proper postage affixed.

When you do this, the moment that you deposit that acceptance into the mail box, it is a completed contract. The person who gave you the offer has then accepted it. The post office is his agent.

(Internal Revenue, as you will recall, accepts your tax return as being filed with them the moment that you deposit it into the U.S. mail box.)

NOW, there is an exception to this basic rule.
Example:

A contract offer may be specified as being effective *only upon receipt of written acceptance in our Home Office OR you pay your mortgage payment which is due in our Home Office in Omaha on or before the fifth of each month.* If you have that limitation stated in the offer, then that is an exception to the mail box rule.

Now, let's talk about
TERMINATION OF OFFER:
This is important to remember: If you make an offer, *you may withdraw the offer* at any time **prior** to acceptance by the Offeree.

Examples:

For general informational purposes, we place an advertisement in the newspaper offering to sell some television sets. One cannot come in and say *I accept that offer* and hold you to it unless you have made a detailed explanation in the newspaper.

You see, a newspaper advertisement is not generally treated as a formal offer but is deemed merely an offer to solicit bids. The exception is if you advertise, *I have a small quantity of dresses in silk, size 14 and 16 on sale for $13.95.* When you detail the specifications, then it is held to be a valid offer.

Jim offers to sell his car to me for $12,300. I write out a check and go to Jim's house to buy the car. Before I can say or do anything, Jim says, *I withdraw my offer to sell my car.* Jim withdrew his offer **before** I accepted the offer, so the "sale" is not enforceable by me.

Let's talk about
COUNTER-OFFERS:

Example:

I say, *I'm willing to sell this acreage for $100 an acre.* Bill says, *That's too much. I'll give you $75 an acre.*

What Bill has done is given me a **counter-offer.**

A counter-offer says this: *I do not accept your $100 offer. I will offer $75.*

Bill's counter-offer is a total rejection of my offer and, in effect, he has made an offer back to me, to wit: *I will offer you $75 an acre.* Now, I can either accept that offer or reject that offer.

Next, let's talk about
CONSIDERATION:

Consideration is the reason, the motive, the inducement, the compelling influence to make or accept an offer.

Consideration is what? It is any act, forbearance or return promise, bargained or given in exchange for a promise.

Example:

A customer slips on your store floor and says *I will accept $100 in exchange for not suing you,* or you may give your customer $100 if he will sign a **Release** which says he will not sue you. And it will be binding. BUT, the customer must be an informed customer. The customer must be aware of their legal rights.

Now, $100 may be sufficient consideration for a broken fingernail but, certainly, would not be logically supportable on a **Release** for a person that broke a leg and fractured a rib. Logic says only an uninformed customer would sign such a **Release,** and it would not be binding in court.

Now, that brings us to the subject of
INSUFFICIENT CONSIDERATION:

When the **consideration** or the incentive to make the agreement is so small that it bears no reasonable relationship to your agreement, then it is **not** binding.

Example:

You offer a $50 reward for the return of your stolen television set.

Three days later, a policeman shows up and says *I found your television set. I'd like to claim the $50 reward.*

Ordinarily, if this were a citizen, he would be entitled to that reward. But because this is a policeman, the generally accepted principle of law says, *No.*

And why? Because this policeman gave up nothing. As a policeman, he was sworn to defend the law. It was his **responsibility** to attempt to find the stolen merchandise and return it.

So, the $50 reward is not why he was returning it. There was **insufficient consideration.** He already was getting a salary that supported his reason for returning it.

Now, since we're talking about contracts, let's also talk about breaking contracts

Let's turn to
DEFENSES TO FORMATION.

When you enter into a contract, you need to think in terms of: *How do I enforce this contract? How do I break this contract?"*

One way to break a contract is to think in terms of **formation.**
Let's go the defense of the **Statute of Frauds.**
This legal theory means that certain agreements are required to be **in writing,** notwithstanding the fact that a contract is an agreement and the written contract is only a piece of paper.

By law or statute, certain contracts
MUST BE REDUCED TO WRITING.
An oral agreement is not sufficient. If the following contracts or agreements are not reduced to written form, then they are not enforceable in a court of law.

1. *A promise to pay the debt of another.*
    The co-signer on your automobile financing. That must be in writing.

2. *Any contract that cannot be performed within one year.*
    I will buy all the wheat that you can grow in the next 18 months.
    That means that it's impossible to perform within 12 months. To be enforceable, it must be in writing.

3. *The sale of real estate.*
    In order to provide a continuity of title on permanent possessions, it must be in writing or it's not enforceable.

4. *The sale of goods in excess of a statutory amount.*
    The amount varies from state to state. For example, one state might say, *Any sale above $500 must be in writing or it is not enforceable."*

    (NOW, the exception to that is if you deliver the merchandise, say, a $700 television set, **and** the television set is **accepted** by the buyer.

5. ***Promises regarding marriage.*** *Marry me, and I will give you Black Acre Estate.* That promise must be in writing.

Remember this point: When we talk about certain agreements must **be in writing to be enforceable, it doesn't necessarily mean that all terms, all** conditions must be specified in detail. **It means there must be a written memorial.** There must be something in writing to support your verbal statements that you have an agreement.

Now, let me share information about **DEFENSING A CONTRACT,** that is, *How to break a contract* or how to think in terms of *enforcing* the contract when you're in the act of forming one, which is exactly what a smart, shrewd and cunning person will do.

ILLEGAL or unconscionable agreements are **unenforceable.**

To illustrate:
1. **Criminal Act:**
    You make an agreement concerning gambling. Most states' laws say that agreements concerning gambling are unenforceable.
    (The common exception is when the state specifies certain gambling activities under **its** supervision **are** enforceable. For example, lotto tickets.)

Example:
A roofer roofs your house and in your particular state, roofers are required to be licensed. BUT this roofer does not have a license as a roofer. Therefore, in roofing your house for compensation, he is doing something contrary to the law. It is an illegal act, and his effort to collect from you is **not** enforceable in court.

This assumes you find out about his lack of license after he completes the job. To let the roofer do the work and then try to "weasel out of payment" is tantamount to fraud or deceit on your part, and you will find yourself defending your actions in opposition to the ***Clean Hands Doctrine,*** which is a legal doctrine that says that both parties must have honest dealings and not unclean hands.

2. **Contrary to public policy.** An agreement that is contrary to public policy is **not** enforceable in court.

Example:
This little boy next door has been bothering my rose bushes, so I promise to pay the father of the boy next door $100 if he will restrict his child to the inside of his house for the next year.
This is an unconscionable act contrary to public policy and unenforceable.

Now let's talk about another defense to the formation of a contract, and that is a **LACK OF CONTRACTUAL CAPACITY.**
Think in terms of contractual capacity when you're entering into an agreement and when you want to break an agreement:

1. **Are the parties to the contract sane or are they senile?**

Senile? Lacks contractual capacity.
Insane? Lacks contractual capacity

2. **A minor.**
Example:
A 13 year old boy enters into a contract to buy a $300 bicycle. That agreement is voidable. As to the minor boy, you cannot force or you cannot pressure legally the minor into paying off the contract.

Now, the minor is in the good position of making you comply with your terms of warranty, say, on the performance of the bicycle. So
the contract is voidable at the minor's option while the minor is a minor.

Note:
Once the minor comes of age—let's say he turns 18—two things can happen: Either the passage of time by itself will act as a ratification of that contract or, Number 2, let us assume that the minor had been making payments of $10 a month to pay off the obligation to the bicycle shop and he continues to make two or three payments after he turns 18 and then decides he doesn't want to comply with the terms and thinks he can void the contract because it was entered into when he was a minor. NOT

SO. His acts after he reaches majority **affirms** or **ratifies** the contract; therefore, it is now by you the dealer enforceable.

Three categories, additionally, are **defenses** to the formation of an enforceable contract: **MISTAKE, FRAUD, DURESS**

1. **Mistake** regarding the terms, regarding the object.
    I thought I was buying your horse over here, your brown horse. We're talking about a different object, the wrong horse.
    That's a mistake regarding the object of the contract and, if it's reasonable, it is a defense to the formation of a contract.

2. **Fraud** is a defense to the formation of a contract.
    You buy a car, and you are told *This car only as 13,482 miles on it*. You find out later that's not at all true. It has thousands more miles on it than what the salesman told you.

    You have been defrauded. You have been the subject of a misrepresentation for the purpose of inducing you to buy that car. By you, the innocent buyer, that contract is voidable.

    However, that's not to say that the car dealer can't say *This is a very low mileage car. This is a cream puff, in my opinion.*

    This non-specific representation is commonly referred to as **puffing** and is **not** deemed actionable in court.

3. **Duress/Unlawful pressure.**
    You have two kinds of duress: a **physical** duress: *Sign this or I'll cut off your ear* or perhaps **economic** or **psychological** duress: *Sign this agreement or I'll see that you get no more orders for products in the next six months.*

    That's duress. The person exerting the pressure or duress will be unable to enforce his rights in court. That's not enforceable.

    Duress is a defense. If proven in court, that's a way to break a contract.

Now, let's talk about what is termed
THIRD-PARTY BENEFICIARY CONTRACTS.
Where the performance of an agreement or contract benefits a third person, the contract creates a third-party beneficiary contract if the intent of the promisee—that is, the person receiving the promise—was primarily to benefit such third person.

Example:
I take out an insurance policy on my life for $1,000,000 with R insurance company who, in return for my premiums, promises to pay to my designated beneficiary, my wife, the sum of $1,000,000 upon my death. That is a simple third-party beneficiary contract. It was my intent in paying the premium and receiving the promise of the insurance company to benefit my wife, a third person.

Now, in classification of beneficiaries, this becomes important in business. If the beneficiary is identified, such as a creditor or a gift—such as I'm making a gift to my wife of the insurance—if they are identified as directly associated with me, then it is enforceable by that person, my wife or the creditor, in court.

Now if someone benefits incidentally—an accidental, unintended benefit—then it's not enforceable:

Example:
I improve my property which, by happenstance benefits my adjoining property owner. I wasn't contemplating any benefit to that property owner and, so, they are not in any position to try to enforce any rights they might have in court as the beneficiary of a contract that I may have made with someone else.

Now, let's talk about **ASSIGNMENT OF RIGHTS** in relation to enforcing and/or breaking a contract.

An **assignment** is a transfer of a contractual right.
A contract creates rights, and an assignment transfers those rights.

Example:
Party A buys a typewriter from B on payments. B, the typewriter company, assigns the right to collect the $500 payment under the contract to C, the bank. And then C, the bank, can come back to me, A, and collect the

money. B, the typewriter company had merely assigned or transferred their contractual right to the bank, who can then enforce the right.

Generally, all rights in an existing contract are assignable, unless they are too personal. As to the personal services of a chiropractor, for example, you don't want just anybody working on your back but only this particular person, the chiropractor you chose. Those kind of duties are not assignable.

If you want to enter into a contract and you **don't** want it assigned to a bank for collection of anything else, that is, you want to block that assignment, all you have to do is write in your written portion of your contract the words, **"Void upon assignment."**

Now, there are several ways of writing these words, but one way that will get you into difficulty and not achieve the result you want is if you write such words as, **"Not assignable."** In that case, the person you originally contracted with can go ahead and lawfully assign the contract. That wordage does not block the assignment.

Now, you may have some rights there that you may want to trace or pursue; but if you write the words, **"Void upon assignment,"** the person you contracted with, if they try to assign the contract to someone else, will be transferring nothing because it is automatically voided. Therefore, that is a way to block an assignment and keep finance companies out of the picture, if what is what you want.

Let now talk about
DELEGATION OF DUTIES.
A delegation is the transfer of the power to perform a duty.
Example:
You go to a lawyer, and you want him to prepare a legal document for you. Now, that lawyer is responsible for personally doing things. But the lawyer, himself, may not perform the mere ministerial duty of typing words in your legal document. He may delegate that task to a law clerk to draft an agreement or to draft a contract and then delegate a clerk or a secretary to type the contract; and then the document comes back to your lawyer, and he approves all the final language.

In a **delegation**—that is, delegating the duty of performing something—the Delegant remains responsible for the performance of his duties. He cannot say, *Well, it must have been my secretary's error.*

Now, maybe it was, in fact; but he is the person responsible.

Only those duties which will **not alter the performance owed** can be delegated.

A lawyer owes the duty of preparing with professional skill the contract in its final form. Again, only those duties which will not alter the performance owed can be delegated.

Now, let's talk about some issues that relate to **BREACH OF CONTRACT,** that is, the failure to perform a promise.

BREACH.

The Plaintiff, the person who initiates a lawsuit, wants to enforce a contract. So, the Plaintiff alleges, Number One, a breach. That means an actual failure. The person that you hired to re-roof your store didn't finish the job. He breached or broke his promise.

Examples:

The lawyer that you hired to defend you in a lawsuit neglected to file an Answer, a legal pleading for you in court, and the person suing you took judgment against you.

OR

The certified public accountant failed to file your tax return on time, though he represented and promised that he would.

OR

Your soils engineer promised that he would run certain soils tests for you before you built your house or new manufacturing plant, and he neglected to do so.

THOSE are all examples of breaches of contract

ANTICIPATORY BREACH OF CONTRACT:

Anticipatory breach means that there has not yet been an actual failure of a promise, but there is a prospective failure which, if it occurs, will be highly damaging to you.

Example:

On reliable information, you allege in your papers in court that the defendant is going to breach, is going to break your contract with him.

If you believe you have an agreement that is in the stage of a prospective failure, see your lawyer, and he can go to court and get a restraining order restraining the person or party that you contracted with from acting further before damage occurs.

DEFENSES

Now, if you have been sued or someone is charging you with failing to perform an agreement or contract, you may want to defend this lawsuit on this basis:

Rescission:

Example:

We terminated the agreement. Mr. Jones and I agreed that we no longer have an agreement.

Now, in order to be valid, that rescission has to be **bilateral.** Both of us have to agree, and we have to agree before either of us has performed under the contract.

Example:

I was going to give the Jeep dealer money, and he was going to give me the Jeep I wanted to buy. But before I gave him the money and before he gave me the Jeep, we agree to call it off. That is a valid rescission.

Release: A discharge from a duty to perform.

Here is how I can defend: I can say, *Hey, I didn't have to give him $1000 because he released me from that duty. I was discharged from that duty. I gave him $300 and he said, "Forget this. You don't have to comply by July 10. You can extend the time to August 10."*

And I said, *"Fine."*

In this instance, there is a release or discharge from your duty to perform by July 10.

Novation an entering into a new agreement with a person which replaces your old agreement.

Example:

Rather than my paying the Jeep dealer $8000 next month for a new Jeep next month, I have agreed with him that I will pay him $8,500 if he will give me a new Jeep and three spare tires next month. That is an entirely **new agreement.**

Accord and Satisfaction:

You are charging me with having broken my agreement But I say, *We got together, and we compromised and settled this.*

In effect, this means that we were in accord with how to settle this, and it was to the satisfaction of each of us, and it is completed. It is over with.

Frustration of Purpose

To illustrate:

We had a contract regarding landscaping.

Example:

Yes, I agree, I was going to pay you $5000 to landscape all around my building out here. However, as you can see, the building burned down. There is no building. Therefore, there is no reason to landscape; so, I don't have to pay for a landscape job that frustrates the whole purpose of beautifying the grounds.

Naturally, the defense of **Frustration of Purpose** has to be raised *before* the completion of the performance by the landscaper.

Discharge by Operation of Law:

Yes, I failed to perform, and I'll tell you why:

(a) **Impossibility of performance *in law.***

I wanted to buy a Jeep, but now there's a new law in my state that says that Jeeps are unlawful to drive in my state. Therefore, I am relieved from my obligation to pay you for a Jeep because I am discharged by operation of this new law.

(b) **Impossibility of performance *in fact***

I am a Jeep dealer, and I'm obligated to sell you this Jeep on the 15th of next month. But now I want out because Jeeps are going to be discontinued in their manufacture. The company that manufactures Jeeps is not going to make Jeeps anymore. They've made all they're going to make. And so it is impossible, it is a factual, physical impossibility for me to find a new Jeep and deliver it to you.

Therefore, I am relieved from by **impossibility of performance** from my obligation to sell you the Jeep.

Now, of course, in conjunction with that, you are relieved from your obligation to pay me the $8000.

Now, when we talk about breach of contract, a **FAILURE TO PERFORM,** let's find out what the legal effect of this is.

Let's talk first about a **Material breach:**
A **material** breach of a contract creates an immediate cause of action, a reason for suing for damages on the entire contract.

If the performance that was non-performed is, also, a condition to the performance of the injured party, it also excuses the duty of performance of that party.

Example:
If Jones failed to maintain my trucks, I am excused from mailing him a check by the tenth of the month. That's simple logic. And that's what law is, commonly, just common sense.

Minor breach:
I agreed to have the oil changed on your car by noon, and I didn't get the oil changed until almost 12:30. That is a technical but minor breach of contract and is not an actionable breach.

NOW, in passing let me mention a couple of things that relate to material and minor breaches of contract.

First, on an immediate cause of action for a **material** breach, there is what is called *Time is of the essence.* If something in a contract says, *It is essential that performance must be completed by April the first by noon,* and if you do not do it by April the first by noon, then that is a breach of a contract, a material breach of a contract.

The loophole to that is if you can show that, in fact, the circumstances are not such that you are materially injured by my failure to deliver by noon when I, in fact, delivered by four o'clock.

If someone just throws in the expression in the contract *Time is of the essence,* it means really nothing unless time is, in fact, important.

Example:
You are a contractor. You demand a supply here on April the first because you have 150 construction workers out there waiting for the material to come, waiting for the lumber, waiting for the concrete and, if it doesn't show up on time, then you have to pay them wages for waiting. In that instance, time is of the essence and is enforceable by a judgment for damages suffered.

ANOTHER item of discussion in breach of contract litigation is **non-competition** clauses in business.

Example:
I sell you my business, and part of our agreement for which I received extra money is that I will not compete with you after the sale.

That usually refers to: I will not compete with you for a certain period of time—say, two years—within a geographical or market area, say, Los Angeles County or Manhattan. To be enforceable, it must be reasonable. Usually, the time factor is more liberal, say, two years or five years, perhaps. But the area is almost always strictly limited to the market area.

If the business I sold you has a market area of 10, 15 or 20 miles from the place of business, then that usually is a reasonable limit of the market, and I can go, say 200 miles away and open up a like business because I will not be competing with you within the established market area of the company I sold to you.

Again, this is just an example of the exercise of reasonableness, of common sense.

If I'm not going to be competing with you, in fact, then it is unenforceable, even though it is a technical breach of the contract.

Now, let's talk about the legal effect of an **Immaterial breach**, a minor, little thing.

An immaterial breach does not terminate the contract, the agreement.

If the promise which is breached is, also, a condition to the other party, the immaterial breach will temporarily excuse the duty of the counter-performance.

Example:

Our agreement says that you will deliver the concrete to my house by twelve noon, and that I will pay you by check at that time. You don't deliver the concrete on time; therefore, I don't have to pay you at the time the concrete was to be delivered.

Now, if in fact you delivered the concrete the next day and there was no real damage to me other than my personal inconvenience—that is, I didn't have 40 workmen standing by waiting for the delivery—this is an immaterial breach. It was an inconvenience, yes, but not a material breach. However, I am excused temporarily from paying you until the concrete arrives.

Now, if you have a breach of a contract and someone is damaged, what's the rule regarding how much you can recover?

The general rule is this: The innocent party to a breached contract should be placed in the position he would have achieved had the other party performed as agreed. In this instance, money damages, as a general rule, are compensatory. They compensate you to cover such things as your loss of profit resulting from their failure to perform as agreed. How much? Your out-of-pocket loss.

NOW, there's another kind of damage that is called *consequential damage.*

Please note these terms: **Damage** is the injury and **Damages** is the money that you can get in court to compensate you for your consequential damage.

In addition to damages under the general rule, the innocent party to a breached contract should receive those damages which arise from the breach and which were in the contemplation of the parties when the contract was formed.

Special losses that were unforeseen are **not** recoverable by the plaintiff, the person suing. They had to have been in the general contemplation of the parties at the time they entered into their agreement.

Generally, the non-breaching party is under a responsibility to minimize, to offset the damage suffered by myself by reason of the other party's breach. If you are the plaintiff suing to get damages, you can't just sit back and let the damages occur and mount up without taking all reasonable efforts to keep the damages as low as possible.

NOW, there is another kind of damages we want to talk about, and that is . . .

Liquidated damages. This refers to provisions stated and specified in the contract by the parties, themselves, to apply in the event of a breach.

Liquidated damages is not something that, later, a judge tries to calculate. The parties have already thought about, for example, what would have if you failed to deliver the concrete by a certain date.

Example:

You have specified that *the concrete shall be delivered by June 13th and, if it is not delivered by June 13th, the party that is bringing the concrete will pay to me $100 a day in damages for every day after June 13th until the concrete arrives.*

Ordinarily, **liquidated damages**—and that's what we're talking about here—are enforceable. But only IF
- (1) the subject matter is such that the damages are difficult to ascertain at the time the contract was formed; and
- (2) the amount agreed upon is reasonable and not punitive.

Consider this example: *$5000 a day until the house is finished and ready for occupancy.*

Now, if I'm going to suffer damages reasonably in that category of $5000 a day and we fix that figure, then it is enforceable. But if one takes a look at it and says, *Well, I don't see how the damages can be more than $100 or $200 a day,* then to have fixed $5000 a day—even though specified in the contract—the amount is unreasonable and is not enforceable in court.

Again, you get back to general logic and common sense.

Agreements will be enforced in court if a judge (and/or jury) can tell what your intent was, what you are talking about, and have a factual basis, a method by which to calculate your injury.

As part of learning what it takes to be smart, shrewd and cunning in your personal and business affairs, you need to devote study time with the following pages titled Contract Law Review.

CONTRACT LAW REVIEW

A contract is an agreement.

A contract is composed of an **offer** and an **acceptance** and **consideration** that supports it.

In personal and professional and business dealings, when a smart, shrewd and cunning person enters into an agreement, when they discuss forming a contract, they think about the terms, think about enforcing the contract, think about breaking the contract, think about the elements and the question of *time is of the essence* and the *mail box rule* and the *limits of non-competition.*

If you want to be smart, shrewd and cunning, this is what you need to do:
Think about, *How can I defend this?*
Think about the statute of frauds, that certain agreements have to be in writing.
Is the subject matter illegal under your state's laws? Is the plumber licensed?
Is this an unconscionable agreement? What would a judge think about this?
Is the subject matter of the contract morally acceptable?
Am I dealing with a minor? Is he about to reach the age of majority?
Are we certain we're talking about the exact same object?
Are the terms certain and specific?
Have there been any representations that might be a little shaky, that perhaps border on the area of fraud or intentional misrepresentation or negligent misrepresentation?
Do I know what we're talking about?
Is there any economic duress here, any undue pressure?
Can the contract be assigned to somebody else?

Do I want it to be able to be assigned?

Do I want to block any assignment?

Are any third parties here that might benefit from this contract that I haven't thought about that may want to come into court and want to enforce this contract?

When you are engaged with someone in the formation of a contract but have not yet put your agreement into written words but are in the process of arriving at an agreement, as you leave that person's office, as you leave the presence of that person, make your parting statement be: *I think we have a deal but understand, sir, this is preliminary.*

That's the key word, **Preliminary**. That always gives you an "out." Make that part of your mode of operation

After you have left the presence of the other person, you can talk it over with your lawyer as to any qualms you may have about the terms of your prospective agreement or contract. But until you've thought about it and before you put your agreement into written words, everything is **preliminary**. And that's exactly what you stated to that other person as your last words.

FINAL WORD:

I want to make a few comments at this time regarding proving your case in court with regard to contractual issues:

I want you to know about what is termed:

PAROL EVIDENCE RULE

(Think of "parol" as meaning "oral.")

Final and Complete

A witness is not allowed to attempt to vary or explain what he meant by certain words in the agreement he signed. The general rule is that a written agreement or contract speaks for itself.

Prior Agreements

A witness is not allowed to discuss a supposed agreement reached by the parties *before* signing the final agreement. The contract speaks for itself!

Parole Evidence Rule (definition):
No extrinsic evidence may be introduced for the purpose of varying, contradicting, adding to or eliminating terms of an integrated (intended to a complete and final expression of agreement) written instrument.

EXCEPTIONS to the Parol Evidence Rule:
Fraud, duress, mistake as to mutual assent.

Example:
1. *There really was no knowing and voluntary agreement because he was talking about cartons of ice cream and I was talking about single ice cream cones, which we didn't understand until well after we signed the papers.*
2. Technical terms and words of art:
   In the computer business, the word "bit" means....
   In the shoe repair business, the word "last" means...

About right now is the time you should start feeling that you're beginning to get a handle on the legal knowledge of Courthouse Secrets that I talked about when you first opened this book and embarked on becoming smart, shrewd and cunning—legally!

Keep reading and studying and reviewing. Step by step, you're gaining the knowledge you need to boost your self-confidence, to rise above any misfortune and, when the moment comes, to win your dispute and laugh all the way to the bank. And you'll love the feeling!

But don't be overly confident yet. Try answering the questions in the following Contract Workshop section.

CONTRACT WORKSHOP

QUESTION 1:
Assuming competent parties and a lawful object, a binding agreement is formed when these three elements exist:
Answer: OFFER, ACCEPTANCE AND _____.

QUESTION 2:
Smith has a flagpole in disrepair. He offers to pay $50 to anyone who will repair his flagpole so that he might fly his flag. Smith's friend Jones decides to fix Smith's flagpole as a personal favor to Smith, intending to not ask for any payment. As Jones is sliding down the flagpole, having accomplished the repair requested by Smith, Jones changes his mind about compensation. Jones asks Smith for the $50 payment. Is Jones entitled to claim the $50?
Answer: Yes or No. _____.
Why _____

QUESTION 3:
Stockbroker Smith tells Jones by telephone, "I have 100 shares of AT&T available today at $20 a share." Jones says, "I'll take it." Has a binding agreement been formed?
Answer: Yes or No. _____.
Why? _____

QUESTION 4:
Smith made Jones an offer. Jones wrote his acceptance and mailed it.
Then Jones decided to call it off and emailed Smith to that effect.
Smith got the email before the letter. May Smith hold Jones to a binding agreement?
Answer: Yes or No. _____.
Why? _____

QUESTION 5:
Smith and Jones exchanged notes providing that Smith would sell his factory and business for $500,000, "Times and terms of payment and method of transfer to be arranged later." One week later, Smith wished to withdraw. May Smith withdraw without rendering himself liable to an action for breach of contractual agreement?
Answer: Yes or No _____.
Why? _____

QUESTION 6:
Broker Smith said to Broker Jones on the corn exchange, "I'll sell you 50,000 bushels of wheat at 80 cents a bushel." An hour later, Broker Jones came back and said, "I accept your offer."
Is there a binding agreement ?
Answer: Yes or No _____.
Why? _____

QUESTION 7:
Labor Union enters into a collective bargaining agreement in which Management promises not to discriminate against any employee because of the employee's membership in Labor Union. Can Smith, a member of Labor Union and an employee of Management enforce the promise made by Management?
Answer: Yes or No _____.
Why? _____

QUESTION 8:
In a breach of contract lawsuit between Smith and Jones, Jones wants to testify about what Smith and Jones talked about before they signed their agreement. Will Jones be allowed to testify about the conversation?
Answer: Yes or No _____.
Why? _____

CHAPTER THREE

Tort Law
Injuries to Person and Property

WHAT IS A TORT?

A tort is a **blameworthy** act by which one infringes upon the rights of another and causes a loss or injury.

A tort is a blameworthy act for which a civil action for redress will lie. You can sue someone in court to recover money damages.

Just as in our discussion concerning promises and agreements (Contract Law) where there are specific elements that must be proved in court in order to win your case, the same is true in lawsuits to recover money damages relating to injuries to person and property, whether it arises from an automobile accident or the unlawful use of your copyright material or the event where you were sexually assaulted and are suing for money damages.

Elements are the parts of the act that determine whether there is a legal responsibility to compensate you, the injured party, for the tortuous or wrongful or blameworthy acts of the person you sue.

ELEMENTS:

Let's consider these acts of Jack and Jill:

Jack wants to kick a football, and Jill said, *I'll hold it for you.*

As Jack starts to kick the football, Jill lets go of the football, and Jack's leg swings free and he goes up in the air and falls on his posterior, thereby injuring himself—perhaps slightly—and his pride severely. Jill is hysterical with laughter.

Jack is upset and goes to see his lawyer. He questions his lawyer:
Can I sue Jill for the injury she caused to me?

And his lawyer says, *Let's look at the elements. The elements of a tort are these, Jack:*

A legally protected right of the plaintiff. That's you.
Jack you have a right to life, liberty and pursuit of happiness.

A **duty** of the defendant—that's Jill—regarding the rights of the plaintiff.

A **duty** is a legal obligation, such as a parent to protect a child, a driver with an automobile having a duty to operate the automobile properly and not cross over to the other side of the street and hit another car.

The defendant's (Jill's) **breach** of the duty, that is, the violation of the obligation that defendant Jill owes, which *proximately* causes a *loss* or *injury* to the plaintiff (Jack). That is, was the plaintiff damaged, either by his personal injury or his property damaged?

Jack's lawyer says, *Jack, we have a problem here. Jill had no duty to you. If you had paid her $5 to hold the football, there would have been a legal relationship, just as you pay money to a bus driver to take you for a ride on his bus. But there was no special relationship here, Jack; therefore, you have no cause of action, no right to sue for damages.*

KINDS OF TORTS:
Let's talk about kinds of torts by classification:

Intentional torts to *person,* that is, one person punches another person.

Intentional torts to *property,* that is, someone smashes in the window to your automobile.

Negligence, that is, the kind of a tort you have when you talk about a careless driver of an automobile.

Strict liability, that is, the kind of liability you have when you have a vicious guard dog on your property

Misrepresentation, the kind of representation when a car sales person tells you, *This car has less than 1000 miles on it,* when he knows the car probably has at least 10,000 miles on it.

Interference with *intangible* personal interests—such as a Hollywood actor being blacklisted—has the effect of interfering with the actor's ability or right to make a living.

INTENTIONAL TORTS TO PERSON
Now, let's talk about the first kind of tort, the intentional tort to person. Intentional torts involving conduct directed against the person are:

Battery. You punch somebody.

Assault. You almost punch somebody.

False imprisonment. Without a right, you confine someone.

BATTERY:
A battery is an intentional *harmful* or *offensive* touching of the person of another.
You can have a harmful or offense touching of another person sexually, such as in rape. Now, rape is a crime, but it is also a civil battery. You have a right to sue the rapist for money damages.

ELEMENTS:
And what are the elements of a battery?
Intent, that is, a volitional act by the perpetrator.

A *touching,* that is, actual physical contact of…

The *person* of another, that is, the touching was in connection with the person of another, either by touching their skin or you touched something closely associated with them, such as the person's hat or their shirt or their shoe. And a *harmful* or *offensive* touching, that is, the touching was either harmful or offensive to the person touched.

Any harmful or offensive touching is a battery unless it was committed with consent or a legal privilege, such as a police officer under proper circumstances having the privilege of touching you to put handcuffs on you when arresting you.

ASSAULT:
An assault is an *incomplete* battery.
An assault is the intentional placing of another in reasonable *apprehension* of an immediate *battery.*

ELEMENTS:
What are the elements of an assault?

Intent, that is, a volitional act by perpetrator.

Was the victim placed in *apprehension* of an *immediate* battery?
AND

Was the apprehension *reasonable.*

Example:
You come up to me with your fist doubled up and shout, *I'm going to smack you right in the nose!"*
 I'm frightened, and I'm apprehensive that you're going to hit me in the nose, and my apprehension is reasonable.

If I throw a rock at a person, only instead of hitting Joe, whom I aimed at, I hit Smith by mistake, it won't matter.
 There is a legal doctrine called **transferred intent.**
 Merely because the object I struck or nearly struck was not the object I aimed at or that I was mistaken as to the identify of the person, makes no difference.

Let's, also, remember that under *Assault* that threats of **future** acts are insufficient:

Examples:
"I'm going to hit you right in the nose the first of next month." That's not sufficient for an assault at this time.
Further: "I'm going to punch you in the nose right now." And before the person can do it, you punch him. Not sufficient.

Words, by themselves, are never sufficient justification for you to hit another person

Let's keep in mind that an *Assault* is a *lesser included offense* of a *Battery.* That is, an assault is an incomplete battery, an almost completed battery.

FALSE IMPRISONMENT:
Another intentional tort to a person is false imprisonment.
Right now we're going to treat this as a civil offense, though we will be covering this, also, under our discussion of Criminal Law.

False imprisonment is the intentional *confinement* of a victim within boundaries fixed by the defendant.

ELEMENTS:
The elements of a false imprisonment are:
Intent, that is, you intend to confine the victim; and there was, in f act, a confinement of the victim.

There is no false imprisonment if a way of **escape** is left open to the victim without peril to the victim's life or limb.

Example:
If I take your daughter and place her on a raft in the middle of a small lake, knowing that she cannot swim, I have falsely confined her. That is, I have confined her, and I have no legal privilege to do it. Therefore, that is a false confinement or false imprisonment.

However, if I confine your other daughter in the same way, but your other daughter is a good swimmer, then I have not falsely confined her because she has a reasonable means of escape; namely, swimming away.

DEFENSES TO INTENTIONAL TORTS TO PERSON
Let's talk now about defenses to intentional torts to the person.

When analyzing an intentional torts problem, ask why the defendant touched the person or touched the victim.

Example:
In professional football or in a football game at your local high school, the players impliedly give their consent to be touched because they know that is part of the game

Or ask why the defendant put the victim in apprehension of a touching.
Example:
Someone comes up to me with a knife in their hand and says, *I want you to take your shoes off,* and I think I'm going to be struck by this person with the knife, then certainly it's within my power to raise my fist and say, *You do, and I'll punch you in the nose.*

I'm permitted to put that person in apprehension from the standpoint of self-defense.

Let's now ask why did the defendant confine the victim?
When we look at the situation, we may see that the victim was in this mechanical contraption, and the defendant put a bar across the victim's chest to hold them in.

In this circumstance, look at *Why,* and you see this is a roller coaster, and the defendant put the bar across the victim to confine them so they wouldn't accidentally fall out. It was for their own safety

Now, while we're talking about defenses to intentional torts to person, let's itemize specific items which a defendant may assert and which are commonly recognized under law:

Consent: Did the victim give consent for the act by the defendant, either express—that is, verbally stated consent—or legally implied consent?

Self-defense: You are privileged to use force, yourself, to defend yourself. Now, you are not allowed to use force if you are the first person to use force; **but** if force is being used against you, you have a legal right to meet that force with such force as is necessary to overcome the attack. Usually, that's viewed as **equal force.**

Example:
Someone attacks you with their fists, you are **not** entitled to shoot them under that bare circumstance.

Usually, there must be a **reasonable relationship** to the amount of force used against you.

Defense of others: You may come to the aid of another person, but you must make sure that when you do that that you are coming to the aid of the non-aggressor. That is, you cannot side with the more powerful side, but you may step into the shoes of the non-aggressor, the victim, and neutralize the situation.

Defense of property: You may defend your property to remove somebody or some person from your property, if they are trespassing and you attempt to get them to leave.
You are not privileged to use deadly force. You may use only a minimum amount of force necessary to eject the person.

**Prevention of crime.
As a citizen, you are privileged to use a reasonable amount of force to prevent the happening of a crime.
Generally speaking, those crimes that you may use some force to prevent their occurrence are **dangerous or violent felonies.**

Let's use the acronym "BARRMS" to help us remember those dangerous felonies:
B—Burglary
A—Arson
R—Robbery
R—Rape
M—Mayhem
S—Sex offense

Legal Authority: You have the right to touch the other person and take them firmly by the arm because you are a licensed police officer or a citizen effecting a citizen's arrest. (See my discussion under Criminal Law.)

Detention for investigation. You may take hold of another person—a suspected shoplifter in your store, for example—to escort them to a private place to await the civil authorities. And for that you have a privilege to touch, in most states.

This right is severely restricted in many states. **If you are a business owner,** check the law in your particular jurisdiction as to what rights you have as a storekeeper. But **Privilege** is generally recognized in law.

Recapture of chattel. Someone is removing a television set from your home or office. You have the right to use a modest amount of force to recapture your chattel.

Now, the force must be reasonable, and you must be in fresh pursuit. I see them taking my TV set, and I'm going after my TV set right now.

Re-entry upon land. This is a minority view, held in some few jurisdictions. In many states this will not be recognized. In some states you may use some force as a landlord to retake your premises and to eject the tenant.

Necessity (Minor force): You are privileged to use minor force under a legal necessity, such as your attempt to escape from a wild animal that endangers you.

INTENTIONAL TORTS TO PROPERTY
Now, let's talk about intentional torts to property.

Intentional torts to real or personal property are:
Trespass to land They entered upon your land without authority.

Trespass to chattel. This is the taking or damaging or your property.

Conversion: Someone assumed dominion and control over your property.

Let's talk about trespass to land.
A **trespass to land** is an *unprivileged* entry upon land in the possession of another.

ELEMENTS:
Intent. A volitional act.

Entry. That is the intentional crossing of a physical boundary line of your property.

71

Land in possession of the victim. You drive your truck across a tomato field. You trespassed on the other person's property. Unless you are invited in to load up tomatoes, that is a trespass ab initio.

NOTE: If the defendant can *justify* his act under a legally recognized privilege, he has a complete defense.

TRESPASS AB INITIO:

If the defendant enters upon the land under consent or privilege and then abuses that privilege by committing a breach of the peace, he becomes a trespasser, and his privilege to remain upon the land is **terminated.**

Example:
You have a party. You invite somebody to come to your party and to enjoy himself. After he is there, he starts a fight. At the moment he starts the fight, it is considered that his privilege to be on your land has terminated as he is now a trespasser.

TRESPASS TO CHATTEL

Now, let's talk about trespass to chattel.
A trespass to chattel is an unprivileged taking or damaging of the personal property of another.

ELEMENTS:
Intent. A volitional act.

A *taking* or *damaging*.

Property in *lawful possession* of the victim.

Example:
A person came into your house, and he threw a rock into your television screen, or he took your TV. That is a trespass to chattel.

CONVERSION (Embezzlement in Criminal Law)

A conversion is an **unprivileged** assumption or exercise of **dominion and control** over personal property which substantially deprives the possessor of his rights therein.

ELEMENTS:
Intent. A volitional act

Has the defendant assumed *dominion and control* of the victim's property?

Example:
As a plaintiff, I asked John Jones to take care of my car and store it in his garage, which he agreed to do.

Now, I go back to Mr. Jones and I want my car back, and he won't return it. He is voluntarily withholding my car. He is now assuming dominion and control over my car. That is **conversion.**

DEFENSES TO INTENTIONAL TORTS TO PROPERTY

Let's talk about commonly recognized defenses to intentional torts to property; that is, if you are charged with having committed a tort to a person's property, how can you defend against the charge?

Consent. Pat my dog on the back, please.
If you ask somebody to pat your dog on the back, you certainly can't charge them with assaulting and injuring your dog, if their patting was reasonable and not malicious.

Legal authority. I'm a police officer, and you're under arrest.

Recapture of chattel. That's my TV set, and I'm taking it back.

Re-entry upon land. I'm the landlord, and I have the right to come back in here.

Necessity and *Emergency:*
There's a fire.
There's a rabid dog.

Now let's talk about a major area of litigation:

NEGLIGENCE

Negligence is the doing of an act which a reasonably prudent person would not do or the failure to do an act which a reasonably prudent person would do, under the same or similar circumstances, having due regard for the rights and safety of others.

Simply stated, negligence is the *failure* to use *reasonable care.*

Negligence is being careless when you should be careful. The test is: What would an ordinary man do under the same or similar circumstances?

If a professional person such as a lawyer or medical doctor or dentist fails to act with reasonable care, that is, also, negligence.

How do we test the negligence of a professional person, since they're not an "ordinary" but specially trained person?
When we look to a doctor, that doctor must be as careful as an ordinary doctor would be.
A lawyer must be as careful as an ordinary lawyer would be. A dentist must be as careful as an ordinary dentist would be.

You will note that the standard is not the exceptionally skillful doctor or lawyer or dentist, but the ordinary and good practicing lawyer, doctor or dentist.

This same standard applies to engineers and accountants and all other persons of professional training.

ELEMENTS OF NEGLIGENCE

A *duty* owed by the defendant to the plaintiff.
That is a general duty.
Everybody owes the duty of being careful, of acting with due regard, of exercising ordinary care.

A **breach** of the duty by the defendant.

Example:
You own a business and customers or persons come onto your business property with your consent. They are entitled to feel reasonably safe there because you owe them the duty to inspect and discover and correct any defects, such as torn carpeting, banana peels on the floor.

That brings into play the third element:
Causation between your breach of duty and the plaintiff's loss or injury. There must be a direct connection: The person injured himself because he slipped on the banana peel. That's the cause.

Damage, the injury that the person sustained.

Those are the elements by which you can test whether or not there has been a tort committed, a blameworthy act for which the injured person may sue for money damages.

DEFENSES TO NEGLIGENCE
The commonly recognized defenses to a claim of negligence which may be asserted by the defendant are:

Assumption of *risk* (by the plaintiff).
Example:
You go to a ball park and you get hit by a baseball, and you want to sue the owner of the ball park.
 The owner says, *Hey, you assumed the risk of being there when you knew you might be hit. You assumed the risk.*

 Ordinarily, that is true.
 However, consider this factual situation:
 You were seated behind the batter's box and the owner had erected a safety net for your safety BUT he failed to properly maintain the net and allowed holes to be in the net so a baseball could come through and strike you. That's a different situation. His failure to adequately maintain the safety net was negligence.

Contributory negligence (by the plaintiff).

Example:

You were talking on your cell phone and were careless in allowing the injury to happen, but so was the plaintiff. He was driving much faster than the posted speed limit. So, the plaintiff was careless, too.

In many jurisdictions this will be recognized as a defense. In other jurisdictions, the money damages awarded the plaintiff will be reduced as a matter of law by the percent of contributory negligence the jury assigns to the plaintiff. (See Comparative Negligence, below)

NOTE: If the plaintiff successfully asserts that the injury was caused soley by the negligence of the defendant, then the defendant may assert the doctrine of *Last clear chance*, that is, everything considered, the plaintiff had the last clear chance to avoid the accident but ignored it and let the accident happen, anyway.

COMPARATIVE NEGLIGENCE:
Comparative negligence means that if you are sued for having caused an accident, the jury may compare the degrees of the negligence between your acts and the acts of the plaintiff and reduce the damages awarded to plaintiff, if any.

Example:

Assume the plaintiff sues you asking for $200,000, and the jury initially comes up with the verdict to give the plaintiff $100,000. The doctrine of comparative negligence means that the $100,000 would be reduced by the negligence of the plaintiff.

If the plaintiff was 25 percent responsible for causing the accident and you were 75 percent responsible, then the $100,000 would be reduced 25 percent down to $75,000.

NOTE: If you are a business person and you are involved in any circumstance in your business which may be in the area of tort law—the customer slipped on your torn carpeting, for example—make sure you take notes and photographs and preserve all the evidence you can, as discussed at the beginning under the subject of Justice section.

SPECIAL PROBLEMS IN NEGLIGENCE

Now, let's talk about special problems in negligence so you will be aware of them.

Guest statutes (non-paying customers)

A person is a guest in your car—as opposed to being a paying customer on a bus.

Responsibilities vary from state to state, but in some parts of the United States you will find that the driver of the car owes no duty to a guest. In another state, the driver will owe the duty of reasonable care.

If the person in his car is paying for the privilege of riding there, or says, *I'll kick in $10 for some gas for you,* then the driver owes a higher standard of care: Special care.

Vicarious liability.

Now, let's talk about a second problem in negligence, and that is vicarious liability. This applies under the legal doctrine of Respondeat Superior/Master-servant. This means that the superior person must respond.

Example:
You are an employee and, in the course and scope of your duties you go to the post office, at which time you have an accident. Perhaps negligence is involved.

If it is—if you were careless—your employer will have to respond and answer any lawsuit, as well as you.

You may well be vicariously liable because of the special relationship between employer and employee.

Survival and wrongful death statute.

(Perpetuation of cause of action)

These statutes have to do with whether or not a lawsuit may survive after the person bringing the lawsuit has died.

Example:
Your husband had a lawsuit pending for loss of business regarding the tort committed upon him by the owner of another business and your

husband dies. The right of action he has will survive and allow you to continue to recover in his name.

However, if your husband was suing because of a defamation of character—and embarrassment—that dies with his death. That does not survive.

Domestic Relations (Husband and wife)

Let's talk, now, about a special area of negligence, and that is domestic relations involving, as a example, a husband suing a wife.

Because of their special relationship, you have special problems, such as a husband may sue a wife for property damage but not for personal injuries.

Another special problem in negligence is **Joint and concurrent tortfeasors** (and Release and Contribution)

This is really a question of terminology.
Joint tortfeasors consist of two or more persons who joining together to commit a tortuous act: *Let's beat him up together . . ."*

Concurrent tortfeasors consist of two or more persons acting *independently* whose acts combine to produce an injury to the plaintiff.

Example:
One car and one truck, independently—the drivers of each don't even know each other—at the same time strike a motorcycle.

In connection with this, we have the special problem of **Release** and **Contribution**, which are terms which have to do with the responsibility of joint and concurrent tortfeasors having to pay separately, having to pay together, or one not having to pay at all if the other pays a judgment entered as to each of them.

A **Release** simply means *I'm out of the lawsuit*
A **Contribution means** *We will share in the payment of the judgment.*

STRICT LIABILITY
Generally speaking, Strict Liability means liability *without fault.*

Where strict liability is imposed, defendant is held liable despite the fact he has done nothing intentionally wrong and that he has not acted negligently under the circumstances.

The traditional areas of strict liability are **Dangerous animals,** such as a wild animal or domesticated animal with known dangerous propensities.

OR

Ultra hazardous activities, such as a company that deals with high-voltage electrical transmission lines or a company that has nuclear reactors.

Now, in discussing Strict Liability, new areas of strict liability are emerging under the law and involve: **Warranty**, Such as the warranty on a new car you buy or a jackhammer or kitchen blender.

Negligence or carelessness is not in issue; that is, the Plaintiff doesn't have to prove fault of the defendant, doesn't have to prove that the defendant failed to exercise due care.

A manufacturer or seller of a product may be *strictly liable* for injuries caused by reason of the fact the product is defective and not fit for its intended use.

Example:
You buy a check writing machine and put it in your office and your secretary is using it in the normal manner, the way it's designed to be used, and suddenly the machine explodes and injuries your secretary and another employee.

The manufacturer and/or the seller may be strictly liable to the secretary and employee for injuries sustained and, also, perhaps to you as the employer who lost the services of the employees while they were recuperating from their injuries on the basis that there is a liability to the purchaser and/or the user. In some jurisdictions, there is a liability which strictly attaches to a bystander who was, say, watching the secretary work.

Responsibility varies from state to state, but these are the general principles of law that apply.

MISREPRESENTATION

Now, let's talk about the tort of misrepresentation.

Misrepresentation is a false representation by defendant which caused the plaintiff to rely on it and thereby suffer a loss or injury.

There are two types of misrepresentations:
Negligent misrepresentation and *Deceit*.

Negligent misrepresentation is a false representation by defendant brought about because the defendant failed to exercise due care in acquiring and transmitting information, such as a stock broker making a specific informational representation to a client to induce them to buy certain stock when that information was not accurate and the stock broker was careless in representing that it was accurate.

Deceit is an intentional misrepresentation by the defendant.
A major issue to be proved by plaintiff is *scienter* or knowledge of the falsity of his representation.
A seller has a duty to *disclose* known facts which will materially affect the value of the item being sold.

A defendant, of course, is *not* privileged to commit a conscious lie or to make a representation in conscious ignorance of the truth, that is, when the defendant knows he doesn't know whether a statement is true or false.
A seller is entitled to **"puff"** his product. He is entitled to make certain exaggerated generalizations about his product.

Example:
This is a very fine car. I'm sure you will have many years of good service from this car.

A prediction based upon *opinion* does not generate liability.

A misrepresentation of a material fact or the hiding of it creates liability to the plaintiff or to known third parties, that is, identified third parties.

An opinion by a lay person creates no liability.

An example of *no liability* and *liability* would be a representation that is obvious, such as, *That car has very low mileage* as contrasted with *This car has only 23,200 miles on it* when, in fact, the speaker knows it has over 40,000 miles on it.

A major issue in negligent misrepresentation is a breach of duty to exercise due care in acquiring and transmitting information.

Now, let's talk about the tort area of **INTERFERENCE WITH INTANGIBLE PERSONAL INTERESTS.**

The torts involved with interference with intangible personal interests relate to *reputation, emotional tranquility, privacy* and *freedom from unjustifiable criminal litigation.*

DEFAMATION

The tort of defamation is involved with the invasion of one's interest in reputation and good name.

Defamation is usually found where there is a *communication* which holds the plaintiff up to hatred, contempt or ridicule or which causes him to be shunned or avoided.

Now, by *communication* is meant publication to at least one person other than the plaintiff himself/herself. That is, to tell a person, *"You're a liar"* is not defamation. To tell a person, *You're a liar* in front of another person raises the issue of defamation.

The traditional standard of defamation is a statement which lowers the person's esteem in the community in general, which has to be established in order to create liability in defamation.

The modern trend is any statement which tends to lower a person's esteem in a small group is sufficient.

Let's now distinguish for our own purposes between *slander* and *libel.*

Slander is a **spoken** defamatory communication.

Libel is a defamatory communication by **recorded** form, such as in literature or a video recording.

Television and radio are generally considered *slander* if it's ad libbed or not prerecorded or *libel* if it is reduced to a script or a videotape or compact disk.

A *publisher* is a person that originates a defamatory statement. That person is strictly liable.

A *repeater* is a person who repeats a defamatory statement. That person, also, is strictly liable.

Now, let's distinguish those two—publisher and repeater—from a disseminator of information, such as the owner of a book store or a news stand. That owner is not strictly liable for the dissemination of defamatory information unless he personally knows of its defamatory nature.

WHO CAN BE DEFAMED?
Any *living* person can be a defamed plaintiff.

An *undefamed* person cannot be a proper plaintiff unless the defamation of another reflects on the plaintiff.
Example:
His father is an s.o.b., and he's just like his father.

A dead person cannot be defamed unless it reflects on the plaintiff.
Example:
Her mother was an idiot. It runs in the family.

A proper defamed plaintiff can be a business or a corporation.
If a business or corporation has had its credit, honesty or business character discredited in any way, falsely, then the actor or spokesperson is liable for defamation.

As a practical tip, when you talk about business promotion advertising, it's poor business practice to talk about the lack of quality of your competitor's product. Your approach should be that your product is a good product or your product is the best on the market.
Stay away from having specific comments about a competitor's product.

Damages for Defamation:

The general rule is that damages have to be proved, that is, a pecuniary loss. For example, your loss of employment or income.

The exceptions are for slander and libel per se, which are found when

1. *There is an imputation of a crime.* You don't have to prove damage.

2. *There is an imputation of a present loathsome disease.*
   No person with syphilis is going to work in my office.
   Or the defamation affects the person in his trade or occupation:
   Again:
   No person with syphilis is going to work in my office"

   Or the defamation relates to lack of chastity for a woman or of homosexuality for a man:
   In six months, she'll seduce your whole sales force. Those are defamatory statements.

Now, let's talk about
ABSOLUTE DEFENSES COMMONLY RECOGNIZED TO ACTIONS FOR DEFAMATION
Leading the list of defenses is: **TRUTH**
The defendant has to prove the statements are true in order to have an absolute defense.

Other defenses:

Judicial proceedings
There is an absolute defense by the participants in a proceeding:
Statements by a Judge, Witnesses and Attorneys. All statements are privileged if they are relevant to the proceedings.

Legislative proceedings
Statements by members and witnesses before the legislature while in session.

Governmental statements

Statements made by major officials in the discharge of their official duties.

Consent
If the plaintiff, himself/herself consented to the statement or procured another to elicit the statement.

Between spouses.
It is interesting here that there can be no defamation between spouses in a marital relationship where the law deems them, generally speaking, as one person and the publication is a consent by the other.

Certain Political Publications
Certain statements made on the radio or television where the Federal Communications Act provides equal opportunity for all candidates to respond.

Now, let's talk about
QUALIFIED DEFENSES COMMONLY RECOGNIZED TO ACTIONS OF DEFAMATION

Where there is an interest of the publisher, that is, the person making the statement. An interest may be a socially desirable purpose.
Example:
To protect his own interest, the defendant reports that the plaintiff stole money, if he believes he did.

Interest of Others
You want to protect your employer from hiring a person that you believe would be a dishonest employee.

Common Interest
You want to protect the group of which the person you spoke to is a member.

Communication in public interest, that is, you make a report of improper conduct of a public official.

Fair comment on matters of public concern

Agencies which dispense news have a right of fair comment, to make statements of opinion on matters of public interest regarding books and plays and movies and concerts.

Now, if a dispenser of news makes a false statement which might be defamatory, they can mitigate any damages by making a timely retraction, a statement of apology and a statement that "We were in error."

And even though they may be liable for damages on an action for defamation, this would not support punitive damages (because that is damages granted for bad faith). So, they protect themselves by making a timely retraction.

Now, let's talk about a new tort, which is **INTENTIONAL INFLICTION OF MENTAL DISTRESS**

The tort of intentional infliction of mental distress is involved with **outrageous conduct** on the part of a defendant which is designed to cause and does cause plaintiff severe mental or emotional disturbance.

In effect, we are saying the defendant went too far. It's an act that goes beyond decent behavior.

Profane or insulting language by a business person to a customer might well constitute infliction of mental distress. But a private citizen to another private citizen? No.

Threats of a violent nature: Would they constitute assault? No. Would they constitute mental distress: They might.

NEGLIGENT INFLICTION OF MENTAL DISTRESS

The newly arising tort of negligent infliction of mental distress is involved with careless or negligent conduct on the part of the defendant which is substantially certain to cause and does cause plaintiff severe mental or emotional disturbance.

Example:
Erroneously informing a person of the death of a loved one, or the mishandling of dead bodies, if the family suffers a mental upset from this.

Now, let's talk about
INVASION OF PRIVACY

The tort of invasion of privacy is involved with the right of plaintiff to be left alone and protected from unwarranted and undesired publicity into matters of a private nature.

In effect, this is the serious interference with their privacy: eavesdropping, peeping Tom, wiretapping, opening mail addressed to another, shadowing the plaintiff.

We have two classifications of citizens:

As to a ***private person***, he has a right to have his private affairs remain private.

A ***public figure*** is news, and his individual privacy is limited.

Now, to be sure, even a public figure can bring an action for invasion of privacy. If the statement publicized puts the plaintiff, the public figure, in a false position in the public eye, then there has been an invasion of privacy.

Or using this public figure's name or likeness for commercial purposes without consent.

You see, the plaintiff has a right of publicity value of his name or his voice or his likeness; and if it is used without his/her permission, it might be a misappropriation or unfair competition. This is an invasion of his privacy.

Now, let's talk about the tort of
MALICIOUS PROSECUTION
The tort of malicious prosecution is involved with the unjustifiable initiation of criminal proceedings against plaintiff by defendant. The defendant initiates a *criminal* action without an honest and reasonable belief.

Malicious prosecution is to be distinguished from abuse of process.

The tort of *abuse of process* is involved with the unjustifiable initiation, generally speaking, of *civil* proceedings against the plaintiff by the defendant.

The defendant used the process service of the court for his/her own purpose. There was no basis except that it was used as a threat or a pressure devise.

Now, let's talk generally about **DAMAGES FOR TORTS**
You've been damaged, and you want to sue.
How do you know the basis for your recovery?

The General Rule
The general rule to support an award of money damages for tort is that the plaintiff must plead and prove actual damage or injury of a kind recognized by law.

Now, we did have an exception there on **slander** and **libel per se.** Let me repeat here the basic provisions regarding those exceptions:
There is an imputation of a crime. You don't have to prove damage.
There is an imputation of a present loathsome disease.
For more detail, please refer back to the subject of **Slander** and **Libel per se.**

Compensatory Damages
Compensatory damages is the term used to describe an award of money in an amount calculated to offset or *compensate* the plaintiff for the loss suffered by reason of the conduct of the defendant. This amount of money will make the plaintiff whole, again. It will turn back the clock.

General damages are damages awarded for pain and suffering.

Special damages are damages awarded for out-of-pocket expenses for such items of expense such as x-rays or for nursing care.

Now, another kind of damages is **Punitive Damages**.
Punitive damages is the term used to describe an award of money in excess of normal compensatory damages.

Punitive damages are awarded to plaintiff in order to punish the defendant for **outrageous conduct**. It tells society, *We won't tolerate this type of conduct.*

Treble Damages and Costs

Treble damages is the term used to describe an award of money in an amount which is three times actual damages sustained by the plaintiff, plus costs of suit, including reasonable attorneys' fee.

Treble damages are awarded plaintiff for injury to his *business* or property by reason of acts of defendant *forbidden* in federal and state *antitrust* laws relating to *restraints of trade,* illegal combinations, and unfair business practices.

These damages are designed to promote and protect free enterprise for the public good.

How do you compute treble damages?

Let's assume the actual damages suffered by reason of loss of business is $150,000. You multiple the actual damages by three, equaling $450,000, plus perhaps attorneys' fee of, say, $150,000 to equal total damages of $600,000.

Because of the enormous awards of damages that are granted in business litigation and antitrust, it behooves every business person to be extremely careful in any act or agreement which has the possibility of restricting trade or which may be classified as an unfair business practice.

Now, generally, we have talked about **a tort being a blameworthy act which causes an injury or a loss.** In effect, you do something harmful—either by act or omission to act—and you pay.

If you physically threaten or strike or confine somebody, you pay for it.

If you manufacture or sell a product which, without fault, injures someone in its intended use, you pay for it.

If you interfere with someone's business or personal reputation or their intangible property right, you pay for it.

If you interfere with a public or private free enterprise system or trade or price structure, you pay for it.

You need to recognize your potential liability.

At this time, I would like you to proceed to the next section titled, Tort Law Review.

TORT LAW REVIEW

INTENTIONAL TORTS TO PERSON
    Battery Assault
    False Imprisonment

DEFENSES TO INTENTIONAL TORTS TO PERSON
    Consent
    Self-defense
    Defense of others
    Defense of property
    Prevention of crime (dangerous/violent felony) BARRMS:
        Burglary
        Arson
        Robbery
        Rape
        Mayhem
        Sex offense

        Legal authority
        Detention for investigation
        Recapture of chattel
        Re-entry upon land (minority view)
        Necessity (minor force)

INTENTIONAL TORTS TO PROPERTY
    Trespass to land
    Trespass to chattel
    Conversion

DEFENSES TO INTENTIONAL TORTS TO PROPERTY
    Consent
    Legal Authority
    Recapture of chattel Re-entry upon land

Necessity
    Emergency:
    Fire, Rabid dog.
    Prevent crime in progress

NEGLIGENCE
Carelessness.
The failure to use reasonable care.
    Duty
    Breach
    Causation Damages

DEFENSES TO NEGLIGENCE
    Assumption of risk by plaintiff
    Contributory negligence by plaintiff
    Last clear chance to avoid by defendant
    Comparative negligence
        Comparing negligence of plaintiff and defendant
        Reduction of plaintiff's award of damages

SPECIAL PROBLEMS IN NEGLIGENCE
Guest statutes/Paying customer Vicarious liability.
    Respondeat superior
    Master/servant.
Domestic relations
    (Husband/wife)
Joint and concurrent tortfeasors
    Release and Contribution

STRICT LIABILITY
Dangerous animals
Ultra-hazardous activities.

New area of Strict Liability: Warranty
    Negligence or carelessness not in issue
    Strictly liable:
        Products liability

MISREPRESENTATION

Deceit
Scienter (Knowledge by defendant of falsity)
Negligent misrepresentation
Breach of duty to exercise due care re information

INTERFERENCE WITH INTANGIBLE PERSONAL INTERESTS
Defamation
Slander
Libel

Intentional infliction of mental distress
Negligent infliction
"Substantial certainty" substitutes for "intent"

Invasion of privacy
Right to be left alone
Exception: Celebrities

Malicious prosecution
Unjustifiable initiation of criminal proceedings:
Example: False arrest (no reasonable basis)
Civil counterpart: Abuse of process

DAMAGES REGARDING ALL TORTS:
All damages proximately caused and compensatory only. Punitive applies only as to fraud or outrageous conduct.
Comparative damages applies in many states.

TORT WORKSHOP

QUESTION 1
A tort is a blameworthy act by one which infringes upon the rights of another and causes a loss or injury.
Answer: True or False _____

QUESTION 2
"The failure to use reasonable care. The doing of an act which a reasonably prudent person would not do or the failure to do an act which a reasonably prudent person would do, under the same or similar circumstances, having due regard for the rights an safety of others." This is a definition of what blameworthy act?
Answer: _____

QUESTION 3
Smith hits Jones with a baseball bat thinking that Jones is Williams. Has Smith committed an assault and battery?
Answer: Yes or No _____
Why? _____

QUESTION 4
Smith enticed Jones into a train's engine cab, opened the throttle and jumped off as the engine started up and the train sped off. Not knowing how to operate the engine or stop the train, Jones was carried along for many miles before being rescued. What tort or blameworthy act has Smith committed, if any?
Answer: _____
Why? _____

QUESTION 5
Ivy Smith was driving along a boulevard in her car at or below the posted speed limit of 35 miles per hour in light to moderate traffic on a warm sunny day when a buzzing insect flew in Ivy Smith's window and buzzed around her under her sunglasses. To protect her eyes, Ivy Smith began

swatting at the insect, and Ivy Smith's car thereafter crashed into the back of the Jones car causing Mr. Jones a whiplash injury to his neck.

At trial when Plaintiff Jones sued Defendant Smith for money damages, Ivy Smith testified believably that "When that agitated bug started buzzing around my eye, I panicked and lost control of my car, causing me to crash into Mr. Jones."

The jury returned a verdict in favor of Defendant Ivy Smith.

Is this a proper verdict under the facts and the law?
Answer: Yes or No _____
Why? _____

QUESTION 6
A culvert on a highway breaks down so that the road is impassable. Driver Smith is going to the grocery story and cannot drive on the impassable road, so goes off the road onto and across the adjacent land of Jones.

Is driver Smith liable for trespass on the land of Jones?
Answer: Yes or No _____
Why? _____

QUESTION 7
Jones is told by car salesperson that "This used 2010 Chevrolet is the best buy on the lot. It has only 12,000 miles on it. It's a real cherry."

Six months later, Jones discovers from reliable source that while the Chevrolet was on the lot at the car dealer, the manager of the dealership disconnected the odometer and used the car for his own personal use for nearly three full months.

Jones sues the dealership for money damages.

Will Jones win an award of money damages in his lawsuit?
Answer: Yes or No _____
Why? _____

QUESTION 8

At a civil trial for money damages based on negligence, Plaintiff Williams must prove his case by what standard of proof:

Answer: _____

CRIMINAL LAW

Unlawful Punishable Conduct

I'm going to talk now about what is important for you to know about unlawful conduct that is punishable by fine and/or custodial confinement.

WHAT IS A CRIME?
A crime is the violation of a law for which a *punishment* may be imposed.

ELEMENTS:
The union of joint operation of criminal *conduct* and criminal *intent*.

Criminal **conduct** is the *voluntary* doing of an act forbidden by law or, conversely, the failure to act where there is an affirmative duty required by law, such as a father intentionally failing to feed his children.

Criminal **intent** is the doing of an act that intends *harm* to occur or the doing of an act with wanton disregard for the safety of others, known commonly as *criminal negligence.*

CLASSIFICATIONS OF CRIMES
Crimes are classified according to the *possible* punishment which may be imposed.

Felony The possible punishment which may be imposed for the commission of a felony is *death* or imprisonment in a state prison or penitentiary.

A felony conviction may be later reduced to a misdemeanor.

Misdemeanor The possible punishment which may be imposed for the commission of a misdemeanor is confinement in a county or local *jail*.

You will note sometimes that the media reports that a defendant has been sentenced to two or three years of probation. That is not a true sentencing. A sentencing is the actual confinement of a person.

However, there are times when a person is given probation on condition that they serve a certain amount of time in custody.

Infraction The possible punishment which may be imposed for the commission of an infraction is minor fines and loss of privilege.

KINDS OF CRIMES
Crimes against the *person*.

Crimes against the *habitation*

Larceny (theft) and related offenses

Other major crimes such as *forgery*, *bribery*, *perjury*.

CRIMES AGAINST THE PERSON
I'll list these crimes, first, and then in following pages will discuss each crime.

Homicide
    Murder

    Manslaughter

    Suicide

Battery (contact)

Assault (an incomplete battery, almost contacting)

False Imprisonment (holding someone against their will)

Kidnapping (holding someone and moving them)

Abortion (the termination of a fetus)

Mayhem (permanent disfiguring of a person)

HOMICIDE

Homicide is the *killing* of a human being by another human being.

A homicide is not necessarily a *crime*.

A homicide may be *justified* or *excused*.
 Justified means a killing by a defendant who rightfully kills another person in self-defense, to defend his own life or a peace officer in the line of duty that brings about the death of a felon.

Homicide may be excused.
Example:
The death of a boxer by accident in the boxing ring or an insane person who happens to kill someone else.

MURDER
Murder is the unlawful killing of a human being with *malice* aforethought.

ELEMENTS:
 1. A homicide (committed with)
 2. Malice aforethought (a preconceived evil notion)
 Malice aforethought is a man-endangering state of mind.

FELONY MURDER RULE (See next page below)
 By the commission of a *man-endangering* act which proximately causes the death of a human being, the defendant is subject to a charge of murder.

GENERALLY RECOGNIZED MAN-ENDANGERING ACTS
"B-A-R R-M-S:"
 Burglary
 Arson

Robbery
Rape
Mayhem
Sex offenses

DEFENSES *NOT* RECOGNIZED TO THE CRIME OF MURDER:

Defense of property
Stay away from my horse or I'll shoot you.
Not recognized.

Consent of the victim
Go ahead and shoot me. and you do.
Not recognized.

Necessity
There are three of us on this life raft, and that's too many of us here for the food we have.
So you throw the victim overboard to save yourself. Not recognized.

Coercion
The defendant shot a person because he was threatened with death if he didn't. Not recognized.

Voluntary intoxication (alcohol or drug)
Voluntary intoxication is *not* a recognized defense to the crime of murder, but it may go to persuade the trier of fact (judge or jury) to reduce the charge from murder to a lesser included offense or second-degree murder.

FELONY MURDER RULE
By the commission of a *man-endangering* act which proximately causes the death of a human being, the defendant is subject to a charge of murder.

Example:
You go in and rob a fast food store and, in the commission of the robbery, someone gets killed. Perhaps you fire a shot in the air but it ricochets off a wall and strikes somebody. You didn't intend to kill somebody, but

robbing the store was a man-endangering act. And because of that act, someone died. Therefore, you can be charged not only with robbery but with murder under the Felony Murder Rule.

MANSLAUGHTER
Manslaughter is the unlawful killing of a human being *without* malice aforethought.

Voluntary manslaughter
Voluntary manslaughter is a death which is brought about by a man-endangering act but with a mitigating circumstance. Yes, you killed somebody, but there was no malice aforethought. It was in the heat of passion, a sudden acting out.

Involuntary manslaughter
Yes, you killed somebody. There was no man-endangering act—such as burglary or robbery—but there was criminal negligence or other non-felonious wrongful conduct.

Example:
You commit a criminal act such as shoplifting and during the shoplifting circumstance you cause the death of a bystander.

Since it was a death that occurred during a criminal act, you would be liable for it; but it wasn't a felony, a man-endangering act, therefore, it would fall under the category of **involuntary manslaughter** by reason of it being either criminal negligence or, in this instance, non-felonious but wrongful conduct.

SUICIDE
Suicide is the taking of one's own life, killing yourself.

Modern criminal liability arises from ***aiding*** and ***abetting*** the act of suicide by another.

Aiding and abetting a suicide subjects the defendant to charges and rules applicable to *murder*. The classic example is a mercy killing.

BATTERY

A **battery** is an intentional *harmful* or offensive touching of the person of another. The touching must be harmful or offensive to the victim.

This is the same definition as the tort of battery, except you may be sued by the victim in the civil courts for damages for a battery on the theory of tort law; and you may, also, be criminally prosecuted by the government for the same act in order to punish you for your unlawful conduct.

ELEMENTS
1. Intent
2. Touching
3. Person of another
4. Harmful or offensive

ASSAULT

An **assault** is the intentional placing of another in reasonable apprehension of an immediate battery.

ELEMENTS
1. Intent
2. Victim placed in apprehension or an *immediate* battery
3. Was the apprehension *reasonable*.

If a person is afraid someone else is going to strike them but under the circumstances no reasonable person would be afraid, then you do NOT have an assault. The standard is what is in the mind of the victim, so long as the victim's state of mind is reasonable.

NOTE: Threats of *future* action are insufficient.

FALSE IMPRISONMENT

False imprisonment is the intentional *confinement* of the victim within boundaries fixed by the defendant.

ELEMENTS
1. Intent
2. Confinement of the victim.

There is no false imprisonment if a way of *escape* is left open and available to the victim without peril to life or limb. The confinement is in the state of mind of the victim. If they honestly think they are confined, then they are, even though there may be a reasonable means of escape of which they are unaware.

NOTE: False imprisonment resembles "assault" in that threats of future action are insufficient.

You could be sued for damages in a civil action if you perpetrated a false imprisonment against someone.

And you may also be prosecuted criminally for the same act.

KIDNAPPING
Kidnapping is the false imprisonment of a person together with a material *movement* of the victim.

ELEMENTS
1. False imprisonment
2. Material movement.

Twenty feet or twenty miles, the standard is any movement which materially increases the danger to the victim.

Example:
You falsely imprison someone and take them three miles away and ask for a ransom. We all recognize that as a kidnapping. Similarly, a man attacks a woman next to a shrub on a sidewalk. That's an assault and battery.

But if that defendant pulls the woman behind some bushes say fifty feet away and in a more secret and secluded place where passersby could not see and would be less likely to be able to help her, the defendant has increased the danger of risk of harm to the victim and would be subject to prosecution for not only an assault and battery but to a possible charge of kidnapping.

Material movement is described in law as **asportation**.

In actual practice, the prosecutor may charge the defendant with kidnapping, even though the movement was a short distance, and then in a plea bargained negotiation with the defendant will agree to dismiss the kidnapping charge in exchange for the defendant pleading guilty to the lesser charge of assault and battery.

RAPE

Rape is the unlawful act of sexual intercourse with a woman *without* her consent.

ELEMENTS

1. Sexual intercourse; that is the penetration, however slight, of the male organ of copulation with that of the female.
2. Lack of consent. (Actual and legal consent)

Traditionally a marriage contract between and man and a woman supplies the consent of the woman, whether she gives actual consent or not. That standard is changing.

In a non-marital circumstance, consent must be legal consent, that is, the woman must be of a certain statutory age of consent. Often that age is 18, the age of majority. That age is set lower by statute in many states, for example, 16 years of age.

When a woman is below the age of legal consent, the woman is unable to give a legal consent. Her statement or conduct which says Yes is ineffective consent.

ABORTION

Abortion is the act of terminating a human fetus.

In our modern society, criminal liability for the crime of murder often attaches if the fetus aborted could have supported itself if removed from the woman's body.

The modern trend is that a fetus at any stage of conception being aborted is a crime, unless specifically allowed by law.

ELEMENTS
1. Criminal intent
2. Application of any means to procure miscarriage, whether physical, chemical or otherwise
3. Fetal miscarriage or termination.
   By statute in many states, an unlawful abortion is a felony.

MAYHEM

Mayhem is maliciously and permanently causing the maiming or disfiguring of a person.

Example:
You bite off a person's finger or ear or scar their face by throwing acid at them.

ELEMENTS
1. Intent
2. Touching
3. Person of another
4. The maiming or disfiguring of a person.

(By definition, the crime of **mayhem** includes the crime of assault and battery.)

CRIMES AGAINST THE HABITATION

ARSON

Arson, at common law, is the malicious burning of the dwelling of another.

By statute, arson commonly includes the burning of a business establishment or automobile or one's own dwelling house or related structure with malicious or fraudulent intent, for example, to obtain money from insurance.

ELEMENTS
1. Criminal intent
2. A burning.

NOTE: Any ignition or charring—anything that produces the slightest bit of ash—is sufficient to satisfy the "burning" element. Mere discoloration by heat or smoke is insufficient.

BURGLARY
Burglary is the breaking and entering of the dwelling or business establishment of another with intent to commit theft or any felony.

ELEMENTS
1. A breaking or trespass
2. Entering the dwelling or business establishment of another with. . . the
3. Specific intent at the time of entering to commit theft or any felony.

NOTE: The "breaking" or "trespass" doesn't literally mean a physical breaking of, say, a window, just the breaking of the privacy of the dwelling or the business establishment. That means, as an example, that you could extend your arm or a pole through a window in order to get Bill's wallet or billfold out of the house. You entered through the use of an instrumentality, to wit, the pole.

As to the "theft or any felony," consider this: It is snowing outside, and you're freezing. So you knock on someone's door so you can go inside and get warm. No one answers your knock, so you "jimmy" open the door, and you walk in. You have trespassed, but you have not committed a burglary at that time because all you intended to do was get in where it was warm.

Now, while you're inside the house, you see a diamond ring, and you decide to take it. Do we have a theft? Yes. Do we have a burglary? No, because at the time you entered the establishment you did not intend to commit the theft or any felony.

If you break into a house in order to kill someone or to commit the felony of rape, that is sufficient to satisfy not only the elements of the crime of rape but, also, the act of burglary.

(Oftentimes in a plea negotiation, the two charged crimes will be reduced to one charged crime in exchange for a guilty plea by the defendant.)

LARCENY AND RELATED OFFENSES

LARCENY
Larceny is the trespassory taking and carrying away of the personal property of another with intent to steal.

ELEMENTS
1. Trespassory taking
2. Asportation (material movement) or carrying away
3. Personal property
4. Intent to steal or permanently deprive the owner of his rightful possession.

Example: Your son takes someone's car in order to go for a "joy ride" around the block. That is not larceny because your son did not intend to permanently deprive the owner of the car with his rightful possession.

EMBEZZLEMENT
Embezzlement is the wrongful appropriation of personal property by one who has been entrusted with and has lawfully received possession.

ELEMENTS
1. Lawfully entrusted with personal property
2. Wrongfully appropriates

Example:
A café cashier takes in money for the owner. That is her job. She's been hired to do that. But then she "ratholes" some of the money into her apron. She takes some of the money out of the cash register and appropriates it to herself. She has wrongfully taken money that as been entrusted to her.

Example:
Your bookkeeper "juggles" the books of account in order to siphon off money for himself.

ROBBERY

Robbery is larceny (stealing) from the person or immediate presence of the victim by means of violence or intimidation.

ELEMENTS
1. Trespassory taking of personal property of another
2. By means of force or threat

Examples:
(a) With a gun in your hand, you hold up Paymore Drug Store and take its money and property from the owner or its agent.
(b) A young school boy takes the lunch money of another school boy: "Give me your money or I'm going to punch you in the nose." The first boy used force or threatened force to take money from the second boy.

RECEIVING STOLEN PROPERTY

Receiving stolen property is the crime of wrongfully receiving property that has been stolen **with** knowledge the property has been stolen.

ELEMENTS
1. Receiving or assuming control of stolen property
2. Knowledge that the property is stolen property
3. Wrongful intent.

NOTE: One who receives stolen property is not acting with wrongful intent if his purpose is to restore the property to the legal owner.

Example:
A police officer receives and takes stolen property into custody as evidence of a crime and in order to return the property to the legal owner.

EXTORTION AND BLACKMAIL

The merged crimes of extortion and **blackmail** relate to obtaining property or value from a person by means of **threatening** to injure or disgrace the victim or any member of his family.

ELEMENTS
1. A threatening
2. Solicitation of value (from the victim)

BRIBERY

Bribery is the solicitation or receiving of something of value for the purpose of influencing the conduct of a public officer (or one entrusted with the property of another).

ELEMENTS
1. An offering or receiving of something of value
2. Criminal intent.

Example:
I offer and/or give an expensive resort vacation to an elected official for the purpose of influencing his upcoming vote on a public law issue.

OTHER MAJOR CRIMES:

FORGERY

Forgery is the fraudulent making or material alteration of a writing which, as made or altered, has apparent legal significance.

ELEMENTS
1. Making a false document of altering a genuine document
2. Criminal intent or intent to make wrongful use of the document.

In this crime, we're talking about such things as deeds, contracts, negotiable instruments, a birth certificate.

Bear in mind that the altering must have some legal significance such as to have a wrongful use or to mislead somebody.

"Uttering" a forged or altered instrument consists of offering as genuine the instrument known to be false with intent to defraud.

When you wrongfully alter a document or sign somebody's signature without permission, that's **forgery**. When you pass or present the altered or false document, that's a separate chargeable offense of **uttering**.

CIVIL "BRIBERY"

By statute, **Bribery** is the solicitation or receiving of something of value for the purpose of influencing conduct (such as the vote of a public official or an official's act which directly affects the public).

ELEMENTS
1. An offering or receiving of something of value
2. A criminal or evil intent.

NOTE: Bribing a private employee, such as an employee of IBM corporation, in order to influence them or to get their employer's (IBM) confidential information, is a civil interference with the contractual relationship between that employee and the employer, as well as being a theft of information (the property of the employer) and may be grounds for a civil action lawsuit by the employer IBM against the person bribing and interfering, in addition to being a criminal theft of the employer's property.

PERJURY

Perjury consists of knowingly giving a false statement while under oath in regard to a material matter.

ELEMENTS
1. A false statement made under oath or penalty of perjury
2. Knowledge that the statement is false (scienter)
3. Regarding a material matter.

Example:
You testify under oath that you ate corn flakes for breakfast when you know you didn't, but no one really cares what you ate for breakfast. You told them the false statement coincidentally with telling them you were up and about at that time in the morning.

Even though you are knowingly making a false statement under oath, it's not perjury in the eyes of the law because it didn't affect a material matter.

On the other hand, if the issue is whether or not you ate any solid food for breakfast, and you said you ate nothing but, in fact, you ate corn flakes, then you have given a false statement under oath regarding a material matter, and that is the crime of perjury.

NOTE: Subordination of perjury is the procuring by one person of another person to commit the crime of perjury, that is, getting someone to lie for you under oath.

Subordination of perjury is a criminal offense.

ATTEMPT
It is common to have someone not charged with committing a crime but charged with attempting to commit a crime.

A criminal attempt is an act toward the commission of a crime which goes beyond mere preparation and comes dangerously close to completion.

NOTE: In modern-day law, there is a merger doctrine which states that a defendant cannot be convicted of both attempting to commit a crime and actually committing the crime.

If in the trial of the case the Prosecution were able to establish that you did, in fact, commit the crime, then you would be convicted of committing the crime.

If the Prosecution could not prove you committed the crime but it could prove that you attempted to commit the crime, the attempting would be a lesser included offense, so you would be convicted of criminal attempt, only.

CONSPIRACY
Conspiracy is an agreement by two or more persons to do an illegal act for which the law provides a punishment. By statute in some states, the crime requires an overt act in furtherance of the object of the conspiracy.

Example:
Three people plan together to rob a bank. Then in furtherance of the object of the conspiracy—robbing the bank—one person goes to a store

and buys a large bag in which to carry the money the conspirators get from the bank.

Let's make a distinction here between a criminal conspiracy and a so-called civil conspiracy.

A civil conspiracy is a term used sometimes to describe an agreement by two or more persons or companies to do an act in violation of trade or commercial statutes, such as two competitors agreeing to reduce their prices in order to run a third competitor out of business or out of the marketplace. This is often referred to as an illegal combination (in restraint of trade).

Civil conspiracies in restraint of trade are often the basis for civil lawsuits for money damages brought by the injured company.

Example:
Company A sues Company B and Company C, alleging that they conspired in an unlawful combination to fix their prices so low that it would drive Company A out of business (an act in restraint of trade).

By statute in some states, the person or company that successfully proves such an act in restraint of trade may recover from the defendants treble the amount of whatever damages the company suffered by reason of the restraint of trade AND his attorneys fees and costs in bringing the action.

PRINCIPAL
A principal is a person who is an active participant in a crime.

Example:
The two of us go into a store to rob it. I hold the gun on the employees, but I don't do anything else. My accomplice, my co-conspirator, removes the money from the cash register.

It is not a recognized defense for me to claim I wasn't involved in a crime because I didn't take the money.

Yes, I did! I was there and actively involved in the crime.

111

And a third person sitting in our getaway car right outside is also involved and guilty. He is an active participant in the robbery taking place, as well as a fourth person who is acting as our lookout to warn us of the police coming.

ACCESSORY
Now, let's distinguish a principal from an accessory, of which there are two kinds: Before the fact and After the fact.

Accessory Before the fact: One who encourages another to commit a crime.

Accessory After the fact: One who aids a criminal actor after the commission of a crime (such as providing his apartment as a place for the principal actors to hide to avoid capture by the police).

DEFENSES TO CRIMINAL CHARGES

These are legal defenses which a charged defendant may assert as to why he/she is not guilty of committing a crime and which are commonly recognized under the law:

LACK OF CAPACITY

  a. Infancy—The charged defendant is too young to understand "right versus wrong" or too young to form "criminal intent."

Example:
The defendant charged with rape is only 4 years old and is physically and mentally incapable of committing the crime.)

  b. Insanity—The charged defendant is mentally incompetent to understand "right versus wrong."

The fundamental case asserting this defense is an 1843 case in England referred to as M'Naghten, 8 Eng.Rep.R.718.

Temporary Insanity

Example: I was so upset, so emotionally deranged at the time that I wasn't mentally capable of thinking about what I was doing or so confused by my temper that I didn't understand what I was doing.

    c.   Intoxication—Because the charged defendant was intoxicated by drugs or alcohol, the defendant was functioning in a diminished capacity and didn't comprehend what he was doing. i.e. was unable to form criminal intent.

    (1) Involuntary—Someone poured alcohol down his throat.

    (2) Voluntary—Got drunk and couldn't form specific intent. I was so drunk when I entered the house through an open window that I couldn't form the specific intent to steal their television set.

NOTE: Voluntary intoxication is not a defense to general criminal conduct. You did the act voluntarily of drinking, so you are responsible for your actions.

MISTAKE OF FACT
Example:
"Yes, Mr. Police Officer, I took this hat from the restaurant where it was hanging, but I thought it was my hat. I see now that my hat is still hanging there. But my taking the hat was an innocent mistake of fact."

CONSENT
Consent is a recognized defense to a criminal charge if the alleged victim knowingly gave you consent to do an act that is unlawful without such consent.

This is the classic defense to the charge of rape. The defendant has to convince the jury that the adult woman agreed to engage in an act of sexual intercourse with the defendant by word (Yes) or implied act of consent (Removing her clothing)

If the female involved is under the age of legal consent—say she is 14 and in your state the statute says the legal age of consent is 18—then the fact she gave personal consent is not a defense because she is legally incapable of giving consent.

Consent is not a defense in a criminal charge of taking someone else's life because that is a crime, absent special circumstances (such as Oregon's assisted suicide statute or the statutory act of a State Executioner carrying out a court-ordered death sentence).

Consent may be a defense for stealing someone's television set.
Example:
Yes, I told Harry, "Take my TV set Home as payment for the repair you made to my hot water tank."

COERCION
Coercion is a commonly recognized defense to a criminal charge.
Example:
Yes, I did sign this check with somebody else's name, but this man had a gun to my head and told me, "Sign this check with the name of Jones or I'll blow your head off." I was coerced into signing the check.

NECESSITY
Necessity is a commonly recognized defense to a criminal charge.
Example:
Yes, I broke into this cabin at midnight, but I waited and waited and no one showed up, and I was lost in the woods and practically starving, so I broke in to get food and shelter from the cold rain outside.

SELF-DEFENSE To protect yourself.
Yes, I did hit that man right on the nose, but that was after he swung at me with the hammer in his hand. I was responding to protect myself rather than initiating a fight.

DEFENSE OF OTHERS (who are nonagressors)—
Example:
Yes, I went over there and slapped that boy across the face;

however, that boy was beating up on another boy that was much younger and smaller than he was. All I did was apply just enough force to assist the nonagressor boy in order to keep the peace.

PREVENTION OF A CRIME
Example:
Yes, I did break into the store in the nighttime; however, I broke in because I saw somebody in the back of the store with what looked like a gallon of gasoline and some matches, and it looked like he was getting ready to burn down the store. I broke in to stop him, to prevent a crime.

LEGAL AUTHORITY
Example:
Yes, I did put handcuffs on this person and confined him and moved him to another part of town; however, I am a police officer, and I was making an arrest. I had to handcuff the man to take him into custody. I had the legal authority to do that.

ENTRAPMENT
Entrapment is a defense.
If the police or law enforcement induce you to commit a crime, argue you into it, persuade you to commit the crime, then you will have the legal defense of I was entrapped. They psychologically forced me to me to do this.

This is as opposed to giving the defendant an opportunity to commit a crime.

Example:
I have some (illegal) drugs for sale. Would you like to buy some?
In that instance, the police officer is merely giving you the opportunity to commit a crime. If you say Yes and offer some money, you have committed a crime. This is not entrapment.

LEGAL PROBLEMS IN CRIMINAL PROCEDURE
(asserted as a defense by the defendant)

If you are charged with the commission of a crime, your lawyer will almost always be asserting these defenses on your behalf, if they are proper to your case.

JURISDICTION

A court cannot act or proceed to act when it does not have jurisdiction.

Examples:
YOU are arrested in Arizona and charged with a crime committed in Utah. The Arizona court can only legally act on crimes committed within its jurisdictional limit, i.e. the State of Arizona.

Perhaps the authorities in Utah will make a legal request to have you extradited, that is, transported to Utah to stand trial.

YOU are charged with committing a crime in 2001. The controlling statute says that a defendant can only be charged with committing that crime within three years of its commission.

Since it is now beyond those three years, it is not properly chargeable. The court lacks statutory jurisdiction to act.

NOTE: A court always has jurisdiction or legal authority to make a determination of whether it has proper jurisdiction to hear the case on its merits.

CORPUS DELICTI
(The body of the crime)

The corpus delicti of a crime does not refer to a human body. The corpus delicti of the crime of arson is the charred remains of a building, which shows that there was a burning and, perhaps, some oily rags and gasoline as evidence showing the building was burned by someone wrongfully igniting the fire: The crime of Arson.

NOTE: A procedural issue in the courtroom is that the prosecution cannot discuss who might have committed a crime until it has established, independently, that there was, in fact, a crime committed.

Example:
You are charged with shooting somebody, and you make a statement to a police officer, "I shot John to death out in the woods."

The Prosecution cannot offer that statement in court against you to show that you committed a killing until it has established that someone, in fact, has been shot. That fact has to be established independently of your statement.

It is a fact that many people confess to crimes they did not commit and/or confess to crimes that have not been committed.

In other words, the prosecution has to establish the corpus delicti, the body of the crime, before it can talk about who committed the crime, you or somebody else.

FORMER JEOPARDY
(But not the old double jeopardy)

Former jeopardy means you cannot be criminally charged in court with committing the same crime a second time, if you were acquitted the first time.

Example:
You are charged with robbery of a 7-Eleven convenience store. You plead Not Guilty. There is a trial, and the jury finds you not guilty. The prosecution cannot charge you with the commission of that same crime a second time.

Now, if during your first trial the jury can't decide (hung jury), the prosecution IS able to try you for that crime a second time because you were not acquitted the first time.

In other words, you cannot be put in fear of your life or your personal liberty twice for the same offense when it has already been adjudicated or decided.

ADMISSIONS

Confessions of a defendant or admissions of a defendant are not enough by themselves to convict a defendant. The corpus of the crime must be shown independently and beforehand before the confession or admission may be used against you.

PROBABLE CAUSE

This is another procedural tactic which can be raised.

Example:
A police officer stops you on the highway and finds narcotics in your car, and you are charged with possession.

Your lawyer may well be able to get the charge dismissed if the police officer cannot state or articulate a lawful probable cause to stop your car in the first place.

The police officer must be able to explain logically in a manner a reasonable person would accept why he stopped and detained you, and that reason has to be a lawful reason.

If there is not sufficient evidence to support his reasons, that is, a probable cause for a law enforcement officer to stop you, then any evidence he may have obtained in a search of your car—such as narcotics stashed under your car seat—will be suppressed by the Court and is not admissible as evidence against you as being what is called "the fruit of a poisonous tree." And without that evidence admitted, the prosecution has nothing to talk about in court except that the officer stopped you. And that is not sufficient.

NOW, I would like you to proceed to the following pages titled Criminal Law Review.

CRIMINAL LAW REVIEW

A crime is the violation of a law for which a punishment may be imposed.

The commission of a crime requires the union or joint operation of criminal conduct and criminal (voluntary) conduct.

A felony is an act punishable by imprisonment in a State penitentiary. A misdemeanor is an act punishable by imprisonment for one year or less in a local jail (county or city).

MIRANDA:
You have the right to remain silent
You have the right to have a lawyer before any questioning by law enforcement officers.

STATUTE OF LIMITATIONS
Statutes of limitations on criminal acts require that charges be filed against a defendant within a certain specified time after the commission of the alleged act.

Examples:
In California, within one year of the commission of the alleged act, except as to murder, for which there is no limitation.

"Statutes" are enacted by state legislatures. For any specific crime in any specific state, you must research the criminal codes in the specific state.

KINDS OF CRIMES: Crimes against person
Homicides: Murder, Manslaughter, Suicide
   Battery Assault
   False imprisonment
   Kidnapping
   Abortion Mayhem

Crimes against habitation
  Arson
  Burglary

Related Offenses
  Larceny
  Embezzlement
  Robbery
  Receiving stolen property
  Extortion/Blackmail

Other major crimes
  Forgery Bribery Perjury
  Subornation of perjury
  Criminal Attempt
  Conspiracy

Related terms:
  Principal Accessory

DEFENSES TO CRIMINAL CHARGE
  Lack of capacity
  Mistake of fact
  Consent Coercion Necessity
  Self-defense
  Defense of others
  Prevention of crime
  Legal authority
  Entrapment

SPECIAL ISSUES OF CRIMINAL PROCEDURES WHICH MAY ASSIST IN A DEFENSE TO CRIMINAL CHARGES
  Jurisdiction
  Corpus delicti
  Former jeopardy
  Confessions and Admissions
  Probable cause

CRIMINAL LAW
WORKSHOP

QUESTION 1
A Felony may be distinguished from a Misdemeanor according to the _____ punishment that may be imposed upon conviction.

QUESTION 2
Defendant Jones goes into a convenience store to rob the clerk inside and panics and shoots dead the clerk while Defendant Smith waits outside in the getaway car.

At trial Defendant Smith may be convicted of the crime of murder based on what rule of law?
Answer _____

QUESTION 3
Jones is taken into custody and transported to the police department and is immediately questioned by two detectives about the facts of a crime they say has taken place.

What rights does Jones have before he is questioned?
Answer: The right to remain _____ and the right to have an _____ before any questioning.

QUESTION 4
Fourteen year old James stops ten year old Billy on the way to school and tells Billy "Give me your lunch money or I'm gonna shove my fist down your throat."

Billy gives James his money but later tells his teacher what happened, and James is soon taken into custody by the police.

a. What crime has James committed, if any?
b. To what court will James be taken if charges are filed?
Answer a. _____ Answer b. _____

QUESTION 5
In the regular course of her duties, grocery checker Mary pockets money from customers paying her for groceries and never puts the money in the cash register for her employer.

What crime has Mary committed, if any?
Answer _____

QUESTION 6
Smith saw Jones, a personal enemy of his, standing with his back to a rapidly revolving cog wheel with the wind blowing Jones' coattail toward the wheel. Smith purposely said nothing and watched as Jones' coattail was drawn into the cog wheel, killing Jones.

Of what crime is Smith guilty, if any?
Answer _____

QUESTION 7
Smith sees Jones approaching him in a threatening manner with a raised knife in his hand and believes that his life is in immediate danger. Smith draws a pistol and kills Jones.

Later, the police investigators discover that the knife Jones was carrying was a rubber toy.

Of what crime is Smith guilty, if any?
Answer _____

QUESTION 8
The standard of the burden of proof to convict you of a life-threatening crime is what?
Answer _____

ANSWERS TO WORKSHOP QUESTIONS

Justice Answers

1. Jurisdiction

2. Grand Jury

3. Federal Court

4. Complaint

5. Voir Dire

6. Stipulation

7. Plaintiff

8. Burden of Proof

9. Answer

10. Deposition

11. Small Claims Court

12 Small Claims Court

13. Execution

Contract Law Answers

1. Consideration.

2. Yes. Jones performed the requested repair.

3. Yes. Acceptance of offer.

4. Yes. The email by Jones refused the offer. By the time Smith got the mailed letter, there was no issue remaining.

5. Yes. A binding agreement must state all terms. Here the terms were "to be arranged later."

6. No. Acceptance must be in a timely manner, which would be immediate on the fast-moving corn exchange.

7. Yes. The agreement between Labor Union and Management was for employee's benefit.

8. No. The Parol Evidence Rule makes prior conversations irrelevant and inadmissible.

Tort Law Answers

1. True

2. Negligence

3. Yes. The fact that Smith was mistaken as to identity changes nothing.

4. False imprisonment. Jones has no known means of escape.

5. Yes. Smith did only what a reasonable person would do under the same circumstance. Smith did not act with carelessness or negligence.

6. Yes. Trespass is forgiven only in an emergency.

7. Yes. The detailed fact of 12,000 miles was false and relied upon by Jones.

8. Preponderance of the evidence.

Criminal Law Answers

1. Possible

2. Felony Murder Rule

3. Silent/Attorney

4. a. Robbery
   b. Juvenile Court

5. Embezzlement

6. No crime has been committed.

7. No crime has been committed.

8. Beyond a reasonable doubt.

SUPPLEMENTAL AREAS OF LAW OF COMMON INTEREST

AARP

Formerly known as The American Association of Retired Persons, AARP is a non-governmental organization and special interest group.

According to its mission statement, it is, " . . . a nonprofit, nonpartisan membership organization for people aged fifty and over . . . dedicated to enhancing quality of life for all as we age." It provides a wide range of unique benefits, special products and services—such as automobile and life insurance AARP is a nonprofit advocate and considered one of the most powerful lobbying groups in the United States.

ADULTERY

Adultery is a form of extramarital sex. It is sexual infidelity to one's spouse. In jurisdictions where legal grounds are required in order to obtain a divorce, adultery—even staged adultery—is a commonly cited ground. Even in cases of separation from one's spouse, an extramarital affair is still considered adultery.

ARBITRATION

Arbitration is a form of alternative dispute resolution for the dispute resolution outside the courts. The parties submit their disputed issues to an independent Arbitrator by whose decision they agree to be bound.

Agreeing to submit differences to Arbitration is an increasingly common requirement before one may obtain services from a professional practitioner, such as a medical doctor. It is a legally binding method of resolving differences in a quicker and less expensive manner.

BANKRUPTCY

Bankruptcy is the legal status of a person or organization that cannot pay the debts it owes to its creditors. In the majority of cases, a bankruptcy proceeding is commenced by a debtor private citizen filing a petition in the federal Bankruptcy Court seeking a restraining order against his creditors. The Bankruptcy Court proceeds to administer the federal Bankruptcy Law by discharging the debtor from having to pay most creditors and freeing the debtor from further financial obligation to the creditors.

Commonly, the Bankruptcy Court will issue a restraining order against all named creditors preventing them from moving to collect money from the debtor such as by repossessing his unpaid for automobile and selling it or from taking money by attachment from his paycheck at his place of employment.

NOTE: When the Bankruptcy Court issues an order discharging the debtor from paying named obligations, it doesn't mean that the creditors will automatically wipe the obligation off their books of account.

An interesting twist: After a bankruptcy proceeding, you wish to buy a house. In checking your credit, it appears that X Company reports that you still owe it $10,000, even though the Bankruptcy Court discharged you from the legal obligation to pay the $10,000. But that doesn't mean that if an escrow is opened to finance your purchase of a house that X Company will submit a claim to be paid its $10,000 still owing. It does mean that the restraining order issued by the Bankruptcy Court is still in effect, and X Company may not "spoil" your house purchase by submitting a claim to be paid its $10,000 out of the escrow account.

Also, certain organizations or companies may file a petition in the Bankruptcy Court asking for a restraining order against their creditors in order to gain time to pay their creditors by "reorganizing" or "restructuring" their debts.

CAREGIVER

Someone who is responsible for the care of someone else who is mentally ill or handicapped or physically disabled or whose health is impaired by sickness or old age.

You are a caregiver if you:

- *Take care of someone who has a chronic illness or disease.*
- *Manage medications or talk to doctors and nurses on someone's behalf.*
- *Help bathe or dress someone who is frail or disabled.*
- *Take care of household chores, meals, or bills for someone who cannot do these things alone.*

With an increasingly aging population, the role of caregiver has been increasingly recognized as important in society. Many organizations provide support for persons with disabilities, including financial payment to their necessary caregivers.

CHILD ABUSE

Child abuse is the physical, sexual, emotional mistreatment or neglect of a child, including any act or series of acts or omissions by a parent or other caregiver that results in harm, potential for harm or threat of harm to a child. Child abuse can occur in a child's home or in organizations, schools or communities the child interacts with, especially by one in a position of trust, such as a school teacher, youth director, coach or religious leader or counselor.

There are four major categories of child abuse:
Neglect, physical abuse, psychological/emotional abuse and child sexual abuse.

CHILD SUPPORT

In family law, child support most commonly refers to a periodic payment made directly or indirectly by a a noncustodial parent to the custodial parent to assist in providing for the necessary needs of a child, such as food, shelter and medical care.

The fact that the noncustodial parent buys shoes or clothing for the child or pays for items of entertainment does not discharge that parent from his/her requirement to make court ordered child support payments.

Further, it is not a legal defense of the noncustodial parent for failure to make child support payments by the fact that the custodial parent waved the payments or said, "I don't need your child support payments." The right to receive the payments belongs to the child, not the parent.

CITIZEN'S ARREST

By law, police officers and other law enforcement officers have the power to place a person under arrest for a suspected violation of criminal law, such as breach of peace or robbery.

In like manner, a private citizen may place another person under arrest for a violation of criminal law, such as breach of peace. When a citizen places another citizen under arrest, the arresting person should summon a police officer to take custody of the arrested person.

The difference between the two procedures of arrest is that a law enforcement officer has a duty to arrest a person of committing a criminal act. He has no legal liability for a wrongful arrest so long as his actions were reasonable.

A private citizen making such an arrest assumes the risk of being wrong and being sued for damages by the arrested person for false arrest.

CONSERVATOR (GUARDIAN)

By law, a Conservator (or guardian) is a person appointed by a court or regulatory authority to supervise a person's financial affairs.
Commonly, it is an appointed Guardian that will supervise a person's health and well-being.

A legal guardian is a person who has the legal authority (and the corresponding duty) to care for the personal and property interests of another person, called a ward. Usually, a person has the status of guardian because the ward is incapable of caring for his or her own interests due to infancy, incapacity or disability. If a ward acquires the need to sue someone in court, the suit is brought by the ward through its Guardian ad Litem—responsible guardian.)

COMING OF AGE/AGE OF MAJORITY

Coming of age or reaching the age of majority is a young person's transition from childhood to adulthood as reflected in the young person's new right to vote, right to marry without parental permission, right to purchase and consume alcoholic beverages, obtain a driver's license or consent to sexual relations. It also is a common determinate of whether a young adult will be prosecuted for committing a criminal act in Juvenile Court or in the regular adult court.

By law, the age of majority or age of consent varies from jurisdiction to jurisdiction.

COMMON LAW MARRIAGE

A so-called common law marriage is two adults living together and holding themselves out to the public as a married couple even though they have not obtained a marriage license or engaged in a civil law marriage ceremony.

Simply living with another person for an established length of time does not create the status of common law marriage.

A lawful and bona fide common law marriage in one jurisdiction is usually recognized in another jurisdiction, even though the second jurisdiction does not recognize common law marriages created in its own legal community.

COMMUNITY PROPERTY

Community property is a legal principle that applies to married partners. In a community property jurisdiction, most property acquired during the marriage (except for gifts or inheritances) is owned jointly by both spouses and is divided upon divorce, annulment or death. Joint ownership is automatically presumed by law in the absence of specific evidence that would point to a contrary conclusion for a particular piece of property. The community property system is usually justified by the idea that such joint ownership recognizes the theoretically equal contributions of both spouses to the creation and operation of the family unit.

Division of community property may take place by item, by splitting all items or by value. In some jurisdictions, such as California, a 50/50 division of community property is strictly mandated by statute, meaning that the focus then shifts to whether particular items are to be classified as community or separate property. Generally speaking, the property that each partner brings into the marriage or receives by gift, bequest or devise during marriage is called separate property (i.e., not community property). Division of community debts may not be the same as division of community property. For example, in California, community property is required to be divided "equally" while community debt is required to be divided "equitably." Property that is owned by one spouse before the marriage is the separate property of that spouse, unless the property is "transmuted" into community property. The rules for this vary from jurisdiction to jurisdiction.

COPYRIGHT

Copyright is the term which describes the legal ownership of a creative work and the exclusive right to reproduce, publish and sell a work such as a novel, a textbook, an article, a musical composition, computer software program, photograph or painting. Any original "expression of an idea" can be copyrighted; however, an idea, title and general plot theme cannot be copyrighted.

Copyright is a claim and notice of ownership. The owner's "property" is protected by the United States Copyright Act of 1976. It protects the owner from others using the owner's work for their own financial gain by using it or adapting it to their own use, such as reproducing selling the song you wrote. A copyright is a legal right which may be sold or transferred to someone else.

To establish a copyright ownership, it is merely necessary to write or print the word "Copyright" on such work. Example: "Copyright by John Jones, 2011." Failure to copyright your work upon publication allows the work to fall into what is termed "public domain," which means that anyone is free to use all or any part of it.

Copyright is established by the publication notice, itself; however, in order to sue someone in court for the use of your copyright work without your permission, you must first register your work with the United States Copyright Office. A copyright lasts for the author's lifetime plus fifty years.

Although the owner of a copyright has the exclusive right to use or copy the copyright material, Section 107 of the Copyright Act of 1976 allows for what is termed "fair use" for purposes such as criticism, comment, news reporting, teaching, scholarship and research. Fair use is a use permitted by the copyright statute that might otherwise be infringing. Non-profit, educational or personal use tips the balance in favor of "fair use."

CREDIT REPORT

Credit history or credit report is a record of an individual's or company's past borrowing and repaying, including information about late payments and bankruptcy.

When a customer fills out an application for credit from a bank or store, their information is forwarded to a credit bureau. The credit bureau matches the name, address and other identifying information on the credit applicant with information retained by the bureau in its files. This information is used by lenders such as credit card companies to determine an individual's credit worthiness; that is, determining an individual's willingness to repay a debt. The willingness to repay a debt is indicated by how timely past payments have been made to other lenders. Lenders like to see consumer debt obligations paid on a monthly basis.

A common term used in a credit report is the prospective borrower's FICO score. FICO scores generally range from 350 to 850. A score at or above 700 is generally acceptable by most lenders to qualify for credit business transactions. A FICO score of 750 to 800 rates the borrower as "low risk" for the lender and usually qualifies the borrower for a low interest loan transaction.

DIVORCE

Divorce is the dissolution or final termination of a marital union, canceling the legal duties and responsibilities of marriage and dissolving the obligations to each other of the parties. Divorce requires the action of a court. The legal process of divorce may also involve issues of spousal support, child custody, child support and distribution of property and division of debt.

Annulment is the dissolution of a marital relationship which has the legal effect as if the parties to a marriage had never married. Annulments are usually granted on the basis of fraud or legal or factual mistake, such as one party was already married to another person or one person had not yet reached the age of majority and was legally unable to be married.

DRIVING UNDER THE INFLUENCE

Driving under the influence is the term which describes the unlawful act of driving a motor vehicle while under the influence of alcohol or drug which impedes the driver's ability to safely operate a motor vehicle.

ELDERCARE

Eldercare is a term which denotes the special needs and requirements that are unique to senior citizens and encompasses such services as assisted living, adult day care, long-term care, nursing homes, hospice care and in-home care.

Elder abuse is a term used to describe a person who abuses or harms an elder person.

EVICTION

Eviction is the removal of a tenant from rental property by the landlord. Eviction may also be known as unlawful detainer, summary possession, summary dispossess, forcible detainer, ejectment, and repossession, among other terms. Nevertheless, the term eviction is the most commonly used in communications between the landlord and tenant.

Depending on the jurisdiction involved, before a tenant can be evicted, a landlord must win an eviction lawsuit or prevail in another step in the legal process.

Depending on the jurisdiction, if a landlord terminates a tenancy, the landlord may be required to give the tenant a notice, commonly called a notice to quit or notice to vacate prior to instituting formal legal proceedings. This is true whether the termination is "for cause" (i.e., because the tenant has violated part of the rental agreement) or without cause (i.e., because the landlord has simply decided to terminate the tenancy). Note that in some jurisdictions, a landlord cannot terminate a tenancy except for certain legally permitted reasons. If the termination is for cause, the tenant may have a short amount of time (perhaps from 3 to 10 days, or longer if the rental agreement provides a longer period) in which to correct the violation. Common causes for eviction include nonpayment of rent or a breach of the lease (such as keeping a pet when pets are not allowed).

FORECLOSURE

Commonly stated, foreclosure is the legal process by which a lien holder or mortgage holder obtains a termination of a borrower or mortgagee's right to retain ownership of his home.

Usually, a lender (such as a bank) obtains a security interest from a borrower who mortgages or pledges his home to secure a loan to buy the home. If the borrower defaults by not making the required payments to the lender on the secured loan, the lender moves by legal process to repossess the home.

FAMILY LAW

Family law is an area of the law that deals with family related issues and domestic relations, including:

* The nature of marriage, civil unions and domestic partnerships.
* Issues arising throughout the marriage, including spousal abuse, adoption, surrogacy and child abuse.

* The termination of relationships such as divorce annulment, property settlements, alimony and parental responsibility, child custody, visitation and monetary child support.

HEALTH CARE DIRECTIVE/ADVANCE HEALTH CARE DIRECTIVE

An advance health care directive, also known as living will, personal directive, advance directive, or advance decision, are instructions given by individuals specifying what actions should be taken for their health in the event that they are no longer able to make decisions due to illness or incapacity, and appoints a person to make such decisions on their behalf.

A living will is one form of advance directive, leaving instructions for treatment. Another form authorizes a specific type of power of attorney or health care proxy. Here, someone is appointed by the individual to make decisions on their behalf when they are incapacitated. People may also have a combination of both.

IDENTITY THEFT

Identity theft is a form of fraud or cheating of another person's identity in which someone pretends to be someone else by assuming that person's identity, typically in order to access resources or obtain credit and other benefits in that person's name.

The victim of identity theft (here meaning the person whose identity has been assumed by the identity thief) can suffer adverse consequences if he or she is held accountable for the perpetrator's actions. Organizations and individuals who are duped or defrauded by the identity thief can also suffer adverse consequences and losses, and to that extent are also victims.

The term identity theft was coined in 1964 and is actually a misnomer because it is not literally possible to steal an identity. A more accurate term is identity fraud or impersonation. In our modern society, identity theft has become commonplace.

KNOCK-AND-ANNOUNCE/KNOCK-NOTICE

Knock-and-announce or Knock-notice is a criminal procedure which incorporates a citizen's rights under the Fourth Amendment of our United States Constitution which often requires law enforcement officers to announce their presence and provide residents with an opportunity to open the door voluntarily prior to a forceful entry and search by law enforcement officers under a valid Fourth-Amendment search where police have a reasonable suspicion that a crime has been or is being committed.

The grounds for a lawful search include:
* Circumstances that present a threat of physical violence
* There is "reason to believe that evidence would likely be destroyed if an advance notice were given"
* Knocking and announcing would be dangerous or "futile"

JUVENILE COURT

A Juvenile Court is a court having special authority to try and pass judgments for crimes committed by children or adolescents who have not yet attained the age of majority.

In most jurisdictions, crimes committed by children and minors are treated differently than the same crimes committed by adults.

Severe offenses, like murder or gang-related acts, are treated the same as crimes committed by adults. When this determination has been made by a Judge of a Juvenile Court, proceedings in the Juvenile Court are suspended and the offending youth is transferred to the regular adult court of further proceedings, such as trial and possible sentencing.

LIE DETECTOR

Lie detection commonly involves the polygraph. Voice stress analysis may also be commonly used because it can be applied covertly to monitor voice recordings. The polygraph detects changes in body functions not easily controlled by the conscious mind. These include bodily reactions like skin conductivity and heart rate.

The results of a lie detection examination are inadmissible in most court jurisdictions as unscientific and unreliable.

LIVING TRUST

A living trust is the creation of a Trust (or artificial legal entity) into which a person transfers legal ownership of all his or her property while still living and then manages the assets of the trust as its Trustee. The Trust is the owner of the assets, not the Trustee.

If the Trustee dies or becomes incapacitated from handling the legal and financial affairs of the Trust, a Succeeding Trustee named in the Trust then assumes control of the Trust and carries out such obligations as are stated in the Trust, such as distributing all assets in the Trust to named beneficiaries after the death of the Trustee.

A living trust is a simple way of providing for the management of a person's estate while still living, especially if incapacitated by illness or mental disease from acting. If the person dies, there is no necessity to use a probate court to distribute his assets because he owns no assets. The Trust owns the assets.

MALPRACTICE

Malpractice is simply negligence by an employed professional who owes a duty of reasonable care to his patient or client and breaches that duty by carelessness, which breach of duty is the proximate cause of injury to the patient or client.

This is the term commonly used to describe the court action when an injured patient sues a medical doctor for negligence in his care of the patient.

MEDICARE

Medicare is a social insurance program administered by the United States government providing health insurance coverage to people who are aged 65 and over; to those who are under 65 and are permanently physically disabled or those who meet other special criteria.

PALIMONY

Palimony is a popular term used to describe the division of financial assets and real property on the termination of a personal, live-in relationship wherein the parties are not legally married.

Unlike alimony, which is typically provided for by law, palimony is not guaranteed to unmarried partners. There must be a clear agreement, written or oral, by both partners stipulating the extent of financial sharing and/or support in order for palimony to be granted.

Palimony cases are determined in civil court as a contract matter, rather than in family court as in cases of divorce.

PRENUPTIAL AGREEMENT

A prenuptial agreement (premarital agreement) is a contract entered into between the parties prior to their marriage. Commonly, a "prenup" includes provisions for division of property and spousal support in the event of a divorce.

PRODUCT LIABILITY

Product liability is the area of law in which manufacturers, distributors, suppliers, retailers, and others who make products available to the public are held responsible for the injuries those products cause, so long as the product has been used in the manner intended by the manufacturer, for example, a steam iron being used to iron clothes.

QUIT CLAIM DEED

A quitclaim deed is a legal instrument by which the owner of a piece of real property, called the grantor, transfers his interest to a recipient, called the grantee The owner/grantor terminates ("quits") his right and claim to the property, thereby allowing claim to transfer to the recipient/grantee.

Unlike most other property deeds, a quitclaim deed contains no warranty as to the status of the property title; the grantee is only entitled to whatever interest the grantor actually possesses at the time the transfer occurs. This means that the grantor does not guarantee that he actually owns the property at the time of the transfer, or if he does own it, that the title is free and clear. Because of this lack of warranty, quitclaim deeds are most often used to transfer property between family members.

A common use for a quitclaim deed is in divorce, whereby one spouse terminates any interest in the jointly owned marital home, thereby granting the receiving spouse full rights to the property

REGULATION '"Z"/SALES AT HOME

Regulation Z refers to sales made to persons in their home in which they are granted by law three days to change their mind and rescind the sale. Regulation Z is a part of the Truth In Lending Act.

SEARCH WARRANT

A search warrant is a court order issued by a Magistrate, Judge or Court Official that authorizes law enforcement officers to conduct a search of a person or a location for evidence of a crime and to confiscate such evidence if found.

An exception to the necessity for a search warrant is usually made for "hot pursuit." If a criminal flees the scene of a crime and a police officer follows him, the officer has the right to enter a property in which the criminal has sought shelter.

SHOPLIFTING

Shoplifting is a term used to describe a theft of goods from a retail establishment. It is one of the most common property crimes dealt with by police and courts.

Generally, criminal theft involves taking possession of property illegally. In the case of shoplifting, though, customers are allowed by the property owner to take physical possession of the property (holding it in their hands or in a shopping cart controlled by them, for instance). This leaves areas of ambiguity that could criminalize some people for simple mistakes (such as accidental hiding of a small item or forgetting to pay). That is one of the reasons that penalties for shoplifting are generally lower than those for general theft. However, in practice most stores are aware of the hazards of making a false arrest and are instructed to be sure there is no doubt (ambiguity) before they make the arrest. Trained staff know the basics, observe the person, observe the item, observe the concealment (theft), keep constant unrestricted contact with the shoplifter, and wait until the shoplifter leaves the store to make the arrest. As for penalties being less for shoplifter vs for "general" theft, in most states there is no specific "shoplifting" law; rather, shoplifting is charged simply as "theft". If the dollar amount of the item stolen is low it is a lower (less serious) theft crime. If the dollar value is higher, it is a more serious theft crime.

NOTE: If the evidence shows that the perpetrator of a petty theft intended to steal merchandise at the time the person entered the retail establishment—such as wearing a coat with small hooks in the lining to hang stolen merchandise—then that person may well be prosecuted for the felony of burglary.

SUICIDE

Suicide is the act of a human being intentionally causing his or her own death. Suicide is often committed out of underlying mental disorder, including depression, bipolar disorder, schizophrenia, alcoholism and drug abuse. Social pressures or misfortunes such as financial difficulties or trouble with personal relationships may play a significant role.

Suicide Prevention: Telephone Hot Line: 1-800-273-TALKt

UNEMPLOYMENT BENEFITS

Unemployment benefits are money payments made by a governmental entity to unemployed persons.

Unemployment benefits are generally given only to those registering as unemployed and often on conditions ensuring that they seek work and do not currently have a job.

WILL/LAST WILL AND TESTAMENT

A will or testament is a legal declaration by which a person, the testator, names one or more persons to manage his/her estate and provides for the transfer of his/her property at death.

In the strictest sense, a "will" has historically been limited to real property while "testament" applies only to dispositions of personal property (thus giving rise to the popular title of the document as "Last Will and Testament"), though this distinction is seldom observed today.

SEE ALSO: Living Trust

WRONGFUL TERMINATION

Wrongful termination or wrongful discharge is a legal phrase describing a situation in which an employee's contract of employment has been terminated by the employer in circumstances where the termination breaches one or more terms of the contract of employment, or a provision in employment law.

It follows that the scope for wrongful dismissal varies according to the terms of the employment contract and varies by jurisdiction. Note that the absence of a formal contract of employment does not preclude wrongful dismissal in jurisdictions in which an actual contract is taken to exist by virtue of the employment relationship. Terms of such a contract may include obligations and rights outlined in an employee handbook. Being terminated for any of the items listed below may constitute wrongful termination:

* Discrimination: The employer cannot terminate employment because the employee is a certain race, nationality, religion, sex, age, or in some states, sexual orientation.
* Retaliation: An employer cannot fire an employee because the employee filed a claim of discrimination or is participating in an investigation for discrimination. This "retaliation" is forbidden under civil rights law.

* Employee's Refusal to Commit an Illegal Act: An employer is not permitted to fire an employee because the employee refuses to commit an act that is illegal.
* Employer Not Following Own Termination Procedures:
Often, the employee handbook or company policy outlines a procedure that must be followed before an employee is terminated. If the employer fires an employee without following this procedure, the employee may have a claim for wrongful termination.

Wrongful dismissal will tend to arise first as a claim by the employee so dismissed. Many jurisdictions provide tribunals or courts which will hear actions for wrongful dismissal. A proven wrongful dismissal will tend to lead to two main remedies: reinstatement of the dismissed employee, and/or monetary compensation for the wrongfully dismissed.

HIGH-FREQUENCY COURTROOM LEGAL VOCABULARY

The retrial is being heard ab initio.
> (From the beginning)

And so it goes on and on, ad infinitum.
> (Without limit)

Plaintiff may exercise the option ad libitum.
> (At pleasure)

The child's mother has been appointed guardian ad litem.
> (For the suit)

An ad valorem tax is considered equal treatment.
> (According to the value)

The evidence will show the defendant performed these acts through Jones Corporation, his alter ego.
> (Second self)

Though not a party, Mr. Jones made an amicus curiae appearance at the hearing.
> (Friend of the Court)

It was a bona fide offer.
> (In good faith)

The Vice-President had carte blanche authority.
> (Unsupervised authority)

The appellate court issued a Writ of Certiorari.
  (To be informed of)

The suit was brought as a proceeding in chancery.
  (Equity)

The obligation is a chose in action.
  (A thing)

An identical case arose in another jurisdiction, and we
suggest comity is appropriate.
  (Discretionary practice of adopting)

The corpus delicti was established by the proof.
  (The body of the crime)

I refer you to Corpus Juris, Volume 12, Page 28.
  (Body of law; law books)

Racial segregation is de facto in some states.
  (In fact)

It's a de jure situation—title without authority.
  (Of right)

The classification of this action is delictum as opposed to contract.
  (A wrong)

The Defendant wishes to demur to the Complaint, and the Court will
probably sustain the demurrer.
  (To stay proceedings)

This is a trial de novo after a mistrial.
  (Anew)

The Appellate Court's parenthetical comment on this point should be
treated as dictum.
  (Collateral opinion)

He was compelled to bring the named document to court since he had been served with a subpoena duces tecum.
>   (Bring with you)

Counsel cited the prior execution of the deed as the basis for his special plea of estoppel.
>   (A precluding act)

The case tile is Jones versus Smith, et al."
>   (And others)

The County Clerk is the Clerk of the Court ex officio by virtue of his office.
>   (By virtue of office)

This is an application for an ex parte order, although I will represent opposing counsel is aware of it.
>   (By or for one party)

Congress shall enact no laws ex post facto.
>   (After the fact)

The case is captioned, "State ex rel. Jones versus Jones."
>   (Ex relatione/On information)

This is a habeas corpus hearing to determine whether the prisoner is being unlawfully detained.
>   (You have the body)

We request this delicate testimony be heard in camera.
>   (In chambers)

Having no funds, he filed his appeal in forma pauperis.
>   (In the manner of a pauper)

The clause is recited in haec verba on the next page.
>   (In these words)

The aunt signed for the boy in loco parentis.
> (In place of a parent.)

An equity or chancery court acts basically in personam.
> (Against the person)

Having no counsel, he appeared in propria persona.
> (In his own person/act as his own attorney)

May I have the filed titled, "In re: Harry Foster?"
> (In the matter of/in regard to)

A divorce suit is often an action in rem.
> (Against all)

I have just read the contract in toto.
> (Completely, totally)

When Plaintiff filed his Complaint, he submitted to the jurisdiction of the Court ipso facto.
> (By the very act itself)

The Court should act by judicial fiat when essential, although lacking specific authority.
> (Let the Court do it)

The Notary's jurat is on the lower left side.
> (Certificate of officer)

The action was barred by laches and never came to trial.
> (Negligent delay)

Counsel filed a notice of lis pendens to warn interested property owners.
> (A suit is pending)

Counsel sought a Writ of Mandamus from the Supreme Court.
> (A command)

The detectives soon discovered his modus operandi.
	(Method of operation)

The issue no longer exists, so the question is moot
	(Undecided and not necessary)

The Defendant corporation tacitly admitted it's guilt by entering a plea
of nolo contendere.
	(No contest)

We allege the deceased was non compos mentis at the time he signed his
Last Will and Testament.
	(Not mentally competent)

That conclusion is wrong, Counsel. That's a non sequitur.
	(False conclusion)

I will sign the order today, but its effect will be nunc pro tunc as of last
week.
	(Now for then)

This is obiter dictum from the Supreme Court.
	(Words of a collateral opinion/Dicta)

The Court granted attorney's fees pendente lite.
	(Pending the suit.)

The return of the corporation was 7% per annum.
	(By the year)

The financial return was $327 per capita.
	(Per individual person)

The rate was assigned as $87 per diem.
	(By the day)

I don't mean to say that is true, per se.
	(By itself)

The autopsy surgeon perform a post mortem examination.
(After death)

The opposing party has not appeared, and judgment will be entered upon establishment of prima facie evidence.
(Sufficient unless controverted)

Undisbursed funds will be distributed pro rata.
(Proportionately)

No permanent appointment was made, so he was engaged as Official Reporter Pro Tempore.
(Temporarily/for the time being)

The parties had no agreement, so we have sued on the theory of quantum meruit.
(As deserved)

You are entitled to have counsel in that a contempt hearing is considered quasi-criminal.
(As if/almost)

It was a valid contract as there was a quid pro quo exchange of property for services rendered.
(Something for something)

The Appellate Court issued a remittitur of record.
(Returning)

This replevin action was brought to recover immediate possession of the items listed.
(Recover)

The doctrine res ipsa loquitur applied where the surgical
sponge was found in the patient's abdomen after the operation.
(Speaks for itself)

We object to his arguing this matter on the ground the question is res judicata.

(Already decided)

We urge admissibility of this testimony as being part of the res gestae and an exception to the hearsay evidence rule.

(Basic facts/already done)

The corporation was also named as a defendant under the doctrine of respondeat superior.

(Let the master answer)

Counsel object to the star chamber tactics of the judge.

(Irresponsible or secret tribunal)

A Federal Court should follow the law of the State when construing the State's status as decisions of the State courts are stare decisis.

(Abide by decided cases)

I was served with a subpoena which commands my appearance in court tomorrow.

(Writ commanding appearance)

In the absence of any showing to the contrary, the Petitioner should be deemed sui juris.

(Competent in his own right)

We ask for a mutual restraining order against the parties in order to maintain the status quo.

(As existent at a given time)

After recess, all parties supra appeared.

(As listed above/before))

The Government charged the corporation with ultra vires acts in that the corporation had no such authority.

(Beyond powers)

I can't recall the conversation verbatim, but I can give you the substance of it.
> (Word for word)

A witness may be examined on his voir dire before testifying to certain technical matters.
> (Competency to speak the truth)

I will accept your case as there has been a tort committed against you.
> (Wrongful act)

Richard Lee Orey

Author's Biography

Richard Lee Orey is a former official court reporter of the United States District Court and the California Superior Court with thirty-eight years of daily courtroom trial experience, including actively participating in over six hundred jury trials and tens of thousands of civil, criminal and domestic abuse cases ranging from personal injury civil trials to criminal charges of capital murder to secret grand jury investigations.

After serving in the Korean War and studying personnel management and industrial psychology at the United States Armed Forces Institute, he graduated from the Chicago College of Commerce and soon became official court reporter of the United States District Court. Later in his career, he was appointed official court reporter of the California Superior Court, where he served five terms as president of the San Diego Superior Court Reporters Association and was a corporate founder and officer of the California Court Reporters Association.

As a Bar registered student, Richard daily studied legal theory and case law one-on-one "in chambers" with California Superior Court Presiding Judge George A. Lazar—a former school teacher—before completing his formal legal education at the Cabrillo Pacific University College of Law, receiving the American Jurisprudence Award of Excellence. He has appeared as a paid keynote speaker in over two hundred law-related educational seminars and as guest lecturer in trial and discovery procedures for the University of San Diego School of Law and the California Western University School of Law.

City of San Diego Mayor Frank Curran's Letter of Commendation for Outstanding Community Leadership is one of many accolades Richard left behind when he retired from the courtroom.

Richard lives in Southern California with Jodi, his wife and life-long companion, and enjoys writing, family gatherings, lake-paddling in his red canoe and leisure time in his rose garden.

The pen and vocal artistry of

RICHARD LEE OREY

Books
How to be Smart, Shrewd & Cunning—Legally!
The Hunt for the President's Wife
The Paradise of Revenge
The Trial Seminar
Courtroom Success

Poems and Recitations
Mother Teresa
I Sit Alone and Cry
A Walk In My Garden
My Nubile Fawn and Me
Be Still and Hear My Voice
I Dream of You
Memories of Another Day
A Lovely Rose
Life Is But The First Part
The Kiss
Oh, Dear God, Tell Me Why!
Yesterday's Mirror
If I Could Go Back To Earth
The Surrogate Lover
Flappers & Speakeasies

Essays
A Letter to My Great-granddaughter
I was Made for You
How to Succeed in Life
The Canoe Principle
Begin Again, Ab Initio
The Pendulum of Life

To enjoy these works and more on line, go to
www.Authorsden.com/richardleeorey

INDEX BY TOPIC

Murder/Homicide 97-100, 103,
119, 137

Negligence 12, 65, 74-76, 91, 138

   Assumption of risk 75

   Comparative negligence 76

   Contributory negligence 75, 76

   Last clear chance 76, 91

Novation 53

Palimony 139

Parol Evidence Rule 60, 61

Performance 41, 48, 50, 52, 54-56

   Impossibility by law 54

   Impossibility in fact 54

Perjury 97, 109, 110, 120

Polygraph/Lie detector 137

Prenuptial agreement 139

Principal/Agent 111, 112, 120 (See
Agent/Accessory)

Privacy 81, 86, 92, 105

Privilege 66-72, 77, 80, 83, 97

Probable cause 118, 120

Probation/Sentencing 21, 34, 97

Product liability 139

Professional malpractice 138 (See
Negligence)

Promise (See Agreement)

Prosecutor 27, 31, 33, 34,103

   Federal 27

   State 27

Proximate cause (But for) 138

Public figure 86

Public policy 39, 48

Puff/Opinion/Representation 49, 80

   (See: Deceit, Fraud,
Misrepresentation)

Rape 10, 66, 70, 90, 99, 103, 105,
112, 113

Readiness conference/Settlement
30, 31

Remand 22, 23, 28

Release 53, 78, 91

Retainer 9, 17

Rescission 53

www.ingramcontent.com/pod-product-compliance
Lightning Source LLC
Chambersburg PA
CBHW032021170526
45157CB00002B/801